Introduction iv
Preface v

❖

Many of the works in this anthology were first published in 'The Broken Fiddle', a new writing magazine, and in the companion pamphlet series, 'New Writing from the North East'. Some pieces appeared first in other local publications and some have been included in national new writing anthologies and read on national radio.

INTRODUCTION: BREAKING NEW GROUND

Tom Bryan
Writer in Residence, Aberdeenshire Council (1994-1997)

This anthology may have been taken towards completion during my term as Writer in Residence, but it was very much the brainchild of George Gunn who used a competition as an effective way to identify new writing talent in the North East. Appropriately, the competition was called 'Breaking New Ground.' That ground has now truly been well-broken and seeded and its harvest should be a long and fruitful one. There is a great diversity of work here; maybe bound together only by geography but there is also a clear statement coming from the North-East, often ignorantly lampooned as the last traces of the kailyard buffoon or couthie chiels in nicky tams. There may be vestiges of the kailyard in this book, but that is not its defining feature. There is also historical awareness linked to modern themes and humour; all rooted in the North-East but not welded to it. This anthology had its beginnings under the former Banff and Buchan District and that is its bias and remit: from the Broch down to Boddam, south to Turriff, west to Portsoy and Aberchirder.

This work cannot claim to be comprehensive. There are many good writers who do not appear here; some of the contributors have only begun writing, while others are widely published.

Poetry is probably the predominant form of expression but, in a land rich in music, storytelling and oral tradition, novels, stories and plays are natural forms as well. I think every piece has something to say - with no apologies: that is the North-East way. Perhaps the book can be seen as a mosaic: different languages, different accents, different origins and livelihoods. I was pleased to be a part of this project which may help remind a wider audience that there are stories to be told and songs to be sung outside the Central Belt.

Tom Bryan, Macduff 1997

PREFACE

by George Bruce

judge of the Breaking New Ground Competition

This is excerpted from George Bruce's commentary on entries to the Breaking New Ground competition. The competition yielded the backbone of this anthology and this commentary succinctly describes the flavour and pre-occupations of this collection.

Twenty years ago, and more recently, the feature of Aberdeenshire verse was in its adherence to Charles Murray as its model and to the ballad stanza: equally the new stories of the period tended to rely on 19th century models, especially those in the Doric. The feature of entries for this competition is a liberation from such influences and a variety of styles and subject matter which reveals that freedom of imagination which allows the writers to be themselves. They inherit the past, but they are not imprisoned in it. The vitality and ironic potential of the Aberdeenshire vernacular is still available, and is used to great effect in many of the entries. While there are a considerable number of effective entries which do not use the vernacular, and while some of these have original and credible story lines, the problem for some is in styles and idioms which suggest the authors have been keeping company with authors of an inferior sort. Even so, in the category of English idiom stories, the best show a concern for serious issues, and challenge for the position of a prize winner. In the case of the verse entrants, the best have heard the accents and rhythms of contemporary writers and have freshness and a living character.

On the Edge ‑ The Broch

George Bruce
dedicated to thememory of Gilbert Buchan
skipper of The Replenish, and to his father, James

"To live here is to live on the edge,"
said James Buchan, 7½ Mid Street,
Inverallochy, skipper of The Buchans,
Gilbert's father, the name being common
but not the man, a'body kent him ‑ 7½.
Ithers micht near company his thochts,
but nae in winnan the exact words,
skipper Joseph Duthie and Love ‑ his T name ‑
amang them, good men a', wha thocht
ayont their trade o' huntin herrin,
or through it, in hope a truth would oot,
beginning frae the facts o' life gien them.
James Buchan's life, handbreadths from the sea,
knew it put at nowt the vanities of class or cash.
Gilbert began from here; respect must be earned.
So he gives his boat an honest name, Replenish,
in hope through work on the sea's face she has
a proper return, though aye in doubt. The edge
aye there. Tae his loons it meant nae thing,
e'en when the sea brocht tae oor feet on the tide
a ba, we blootered aboot the sands or nichtfa
wioot a thocht, for a'thing was in its richt place ‑
the sea, the sands, the South Kirk spire, the links
wi room eneugh for 'the winds o' heiven', as the minister
pit it, tae blaw and howl hine awa ayont the bents,
owre sheenan fields o' corn tae Mormond Hill that tell't

---

footnote ‑ 'The Broch' is a local name for Fraserburgh

the boats whether or no their landfall was gweed.
Miles awa agin the dark hill the gryte horse
shined oot fite, steen by steen a' fite,
laid doon een agin the tither: that big,
the horse, tae walk it roon, heid tae tail,
syne back, half wey yer belly's tellin,
"It's supper time:" and aye there, they say,
'frae time memorial' or the like o' that.
The meen cam up and the tide gaed oot
and the sands were as braid as ten
fitba pitches, and the inshore fishers
wi graips diggin the sands for sanle
for bait, and his yet at oor ba game
or they cried tae his tae help the wark.
As the sanle leapt oor hand's flasht,
but they, like lichtnin back tae their
sand hame, but again an again the graips
flung up sods o' sand and his loons catcht
the sma fish in the air or they dove,
like they were siller needles richt through
thon thick sog oot o' sicht and deep doon
and never seen again. Syne we ran for hame.

Home: bed: nor-east corner: night winds beat
about the granite house. The lighthouse beam
stalks the room, is blunted on the walls,
sweeps off, and in the black dark
in sea's far-off roar, I sleep deep.
Morning - white light swims about the town.
The church spire at the top of our street
is encased in blue. The Central Public School,
encased in blue, waits for me. A white gull,
bead-eyed, sits on a lamp-post, out-stares me.
In my schoolbag is learning. It weighs one ton.

Saturday: he handed me the reins on that icy
morning at 2 Victoria Street as the horse
lolloped free from Mrs McWhirter's milk delivery.
I smelt its warm leathery hide, one hand on one
big tin milk can as I stood between the two,
blowing frost like our horse, Meg, who
snorted into the air as we banged and clanged
and struck fire from the metals in the street.
Under the boards the road ran furiously
as we lifted off. Not since the chariot of the Lord
came like a whirlwind was seen such splendour
as we flew in Jim Baird's milk cairt that day.
From below my grandfather's shovel beard
shouted: "Praise the Lord!" Nothing new
in that. In these days miracles
were as common as tatties and herrin'.

The first tomorrow for me began that day,
the first time my father took me, age 7 years,
to Bruce's Look-Out. It was the first time
I saw the edge. The stair in the big, dark shed,
went up and up owre a white mountain o' saut,
syne a ladder, syne a trap-door, syne oot.
Blint wi licht the cauld sun brak on my heid,
and me tellt: "Scan the horizon." (I had nae mind
o' meetin that word afore. Nae doot it's in the school bag.)
It was seven in the morning: "What do you see?
Look to the horizon. See how it runs near round us.
Look east, now nor-nor east." And I saw nothing
but the sea. Then I saw the endless dark line
drawn by God that separates sea from sky.
"Look again," he said, and I saw come up
from the drowned world under the sea a mast,
a funnel, a boat. "I see a boat!" "Low

or high on the water?" I couldna tell, then
others cam. Syne I saw first one low on the water,
then another and another. Come time clouds of gulls
were about each boat. All this I said to my father.
And he said: "Right, we'll go." And sic a girnin',
an yammerin an chantin, "forty bob, forty, forty,
fifty bob, fifty, fifty, fifty," sic a barkin
an' growlin' like dogs owre meat, deaved my lugs,
in the mart that I was deef as deef Burke
the boxer. It was heiven tae get oot an smell
the tar and ile an saut at the pier heid ootbye.
Come nicht an me in bed, and the herrin quines
yet at the guttin and me hearing the sweetest
soonds ever sangs made as thae heilan deems sang
wi words I kent nae o'. I hearkened or I was asleep.

"Ye're a grander," glowered the fisher loon
at me and I glowered back. I never thocht
ither than the Broch loon I wis like ither loons.
'The rocket's up.' Bang, bang it gaed and his
at squeel and a'body doon the streets gan gyte
tae mak the herbour. Force 9 gale and a boat
in trouble, and afore we're there the lifeboat's awa.
But na, the lifeboat's at the herbour mou witin,
hidin' in ahint the lea o' the north breakwater,
and we kent in the open sea it would be a deathboat.
So it wited and a' the folk wited, and I cam up on
the fisher loon, and his thegither threided the crood
on the Sooth Pier, and at the heid o't,
(faur eence I had catcht a conger eel)
we grippit a chine at the wa, or we'd
been blawn awa tae kingdom come. And mair
and mair folk gaithert. By the mart, hauden close,
weemen frae the Deep Sea Fishermen's Mission,

at the ready wi blankets, hot tea, dry claes,
for them near droont by the watter, and at haund
an ambulance, and fishermen by the boats tethered,
but aye creakin and groanin, for there
was nae stoppin the pouer o' that watter.
The hail toon wis there, a'body
frae granders in Strichen Road to Puddlestinkers -
a' them maistly eeseless folk, Curran Bun Chalmers,
(Champion Prize Winner, Black Bun Competition, London.)
Butcher Macfarlane, Macdonald the Grocer, and oor
school teacher, and a hantle ithers - but a' witin,
quaet, and naething tae see but watter -
heich hills o't thrashin ootside the herbour mou,
lumps o' watter loupin the breakwater and ower
the tap o' the herbour beacon that ends the steen wa.
And his! - we're starin oor een oot stracht
afore's - sometimes nae sky, jist black watter.
Stare we micht hopin for sicht o' somethin
that meth be boat, but naething. Then sudden
she's there. Sudden she's gone aneath a wall o' watter,
and again she's there, that near I saw the FR
on her, then gone. This time nae come back,
finished, I thocht, but na, she's heich
on tap o' a wave that maun carry her stracht on,
aye and be smashed tae bits on the beacon wa.
The skipper steers her clear o't and noo
she's richt in mid-channel. We haud oor breath -
a'body, and the lifeboat settles a meenit atween
beacon and pier, but nae eese, the cross-wave
catcht the Golden Harvest - say I thocht her name -
and swept awa oor hope. Still we wited, still
stared across the watters gettin dark.
And she was there further oot, syne doon, syne
up again, syne ae moment at the herbour mou,

her bow pints stracht at his, at the Sooth Pier heid!
The skipper kent a'thing, kent the shore wave's
back-wash and, bidin his time, kent it, and drove
the boatie through: and a' the folk cheerin
and greetin and dancin, and haudin een till
anither wioot a thocht, wioot a care if he
was Puddlestinker or e'en cam fae Peterheid.

'Not in the storm but in a calm night
and the stars shining down; the vast expanse
of waters, throws his thought back on fishermen.
He is in another world separated and isolated.
To live here is to live on the edge.'*

---

*James Buchan spoke these words in conversation for the
Scottish Home Service of the BBC

The Herbour Wa, Macduff:
The Fiddle, Banff [for George Gunn]

George Bruce

The wa - the face o blunt rebuttal -
sea's girn, yelloch, yammer, snash, greet
an the thunner that wud smore a - this
the wa took on, whiles the squat beacon licht
signalled hope fae its steen stack tae boats
storm-driven, that, but for it, meth stravaig
heid-on tae wa, an that's an en o't,
an them aboard. Exac timin, steady hauns, keen ee,
The Provider wi a wecht o haddock, cod, ling, sole,
twa monk fish, an a conger we cud duin wioot,
catcht saxty mile nor-nor-east Kinnaird,
the nor wun at her stern heids in atween the gap,
nae a thocht, nae a doot at the rin-in, driven
bi thon hard race. They're for hame, diesel pooer,
as the boats, steam an sail, through a the years.

An up the brae in years lan syne
on the green, green girss o Banff O,
Macpherson jigged an played his spring
aneath the gallows tree O!
It soondit oot sae fresh an free
in caller air that's born at sea,
that's blawn some hame, an mony a one
its blast had taen tae kingdom come.
It soondit oot a sprightly tune
or the cheatin clock stapt fat his rune.
He took the fiddle in his haunds
an brak its back, syne stiff he stands.
The soul flew oot, the sang's awa,
lost in the cauldrif wun an snaw,
but far ayont the watters' mell,
like soon soons oot in a curly shell
folk hearken yet tae fit's nae there,
for them the sang's for evermair.

The Flitting

Ian Morrison

The car in front of them was the last to get
through the lights before they turned red.
"Shite!"

He leaned forward and peered through the van's
windscreen, which was, despite the wipers' continual
action, being left smeared by the spray thrown up by the
late afternoon traffic. The grey, darkening late afternoon,
early winter's sky. His hands gripped the cold textured
vinyl of the front seats as he kept his balance on whatever
box of his belongings he was sitting. The car in front, a
shiny, slick-black 4 x 4 with Dutch plates, was hardly
thirty yards ahead, stuck at the back of the queue formed
behind the next set of lights. There was a bank on that
corner; he wondered for a moment whether he'd be able
to nip out to get some money from the Cashline, to save
George coming back into town with him to get paid.
But when he put his hand to his jeans' back pocket, where
he always put the little grey plastic wallet that held his
cards, he discovered that he hadn't put them there today.
There was a long moment of panic, a tight, hot sense of
horror - he hadn't enough cash on him: how could he
pay George? - before he put his hand to his jacket's breast
pocket and remembered zipping them in there for safety's
sake before they'd begun loading the van. He'd been
putting on weight; his jeans were feeling that bit tighter.

"Aye, aye," muttered George, who'd eventually decided
to slip the van out of gear and was pulling on the
handbrake. George Street has three sets of traffic lights
in quick succession between the Causewayend and St.
Machar Drive junctions; they always seem to work in
unison, with long pauses between changes. Arrive at

the wrong time, and it can seem to take an age to get through them. He'd himself once, to one of his lecturers, offered the drive through this part of Aberdeen as a definition in frustration.

"These next lights always work together," he said.

George didn't reply, but stretched his heavy hands back towards the van's roof. His chins uncorrugated as he put back his head and bellowed out what would have been a sigh of gratitude at being allowed to move.

"Noisy sod," grunted Scott. He was supposedly some kind of pal of George's, but he looked nearer his own age and hadn't said much to either of them all day. George was in fact splitting what he was to get paid for the flit with the boy, who hadn't long started working at the same engineering supply firm and had two or three times already complained about how it was the older men, the ones with families, who were usually given any overtime on the go. Most of the older men then wrote him off as being a pain in the arse, except for George, who'd taken him from the warehouse two or three times to help with bigger deliveries and had found him willing to work without complaining. He thought he'd give the boy the chance to make some extra money. Today, though, most of Scott's mind was on the other way he could have spent his day off. His girlfriend had just moved into a flat in Union Grove. Her room, which she had to herself, had a big double bed. And here he was helping a bloody student flit.

"Fit way are in such a hurry for anyway?" asked George. His voice squeezed through the effort he was putting in at the end of his stretch.

"I'm supposed to be visiting someone after I finish moving in."

He'd almost said "flitting", but had decided against it. He'd caught himself being worried about being thought of as being condescending - a student, using the same language as a friend of his dad's, someone just off the fairm; even though, three years before, he would have used the word automatically, without having thought of thinking of using any other, because he'd been just off the fairm himself. And George had been off half his life, and he'd known him most of his.

Not that he was a student any longer, either. But nobody at home knew that yet.

George settled himself back into the driver's seat, twisting noisily against the vinyl.

"And what gender might this 'somebody' be, Jamie?"

Jamie smiled at the big man's mock formality, but was disconcerted to feel himself blushing deeply.

"It's a quine," announced Scott. The bam, he thought. And he thinks he's above us.

"By Christ, I think you're right, Scottie. The randy young bugger winna even take the time to unpack but he's off after his oats."

"I don't think so." What he took to be Scott's scorn at his blush had stung him, and he fought to keep his voice steady, as a match for the smile. To enter into the spirit. "Her husband's a black belt," he said.

George raised his hands in mock horror, then brought them down loudly onto the steering wheel. "Just wait till I tell the boy's faither about this," he exclaimed to Scott. "Messing around with mairried women! At his age!" He half turned in his seat. "Jamie," he said solemnly, "you'll never see 21."

"Nae if the boy's a black belt," sniggered Scott.

"Take it from me," intoned George before pausing. "You're safer exercising yourself three times a day, like Scottie here does. Look at the muscles on the boy!" He grabbed Scott's biceps and pushed his thick fingertips deep into the muscle. Scott tried to twist away, rising off the seat as he levered himself against the door.

"Let go!" he yelled, his voice thick with the pain.

"What muscles you've got in that airm, min," said George, quite evenly. He felt the boy's biceps distend under the pressure he was putting behind it. Serves the sniggering wee shite right, he thought. I can see how you built up your stamina before your quine arrived on the scene.

A horn blasted behind them. George released Scott's arm.

"Lights have changed," Jamie said.

"Well observed, Jamie boy. Now hark to that." George was leaning over, speaking close into Scott's ear as the boy, gasping, grasped his bruised upper arm. "There's a laddie your own age who manages to keep his mind on higher things." He straightened, with only a faint smile, booted the clutch, forced the van noisily into gear, released the handbrake and tried to ease it forward. The stacked load of Jamie's boxed possessions shifted slightly behind him as the van juddered forward.

"Bloody clutch," said George. His tone kept the same evenness, but Jamie could sense that his attention had returned to his work.

"Bloody van mair like," muttered Scott. "Thing's fucked."

"Less of the language."

They drove on for a spell in silence. They made it through the next set of lights without stopping. Just beyond them, George slowed to let someone out, across the flow of traffic, from a junction on his left. They had to wait a moment before the driver, a middle-aged woman, managed to join her lane. She didn't acknowledge George. George didn't comment. Scott looked fixedly out his side window.

To take his mind from the tension building in front, Jamie made himself concentrate, as best as he could through the dirty windscreen, on the familiar George Street sights. The old cattle mart, boarded up and decaying, with the remains of assorted weather-destroyed posters clinging to its slatted exterior fence like giant dandruff scales. The Northern Hotel, with its unkempt liner-style facade and the stuffed, top-hatted brown bear lurking inside the lounge bar door. The grey tenements, with the stainless steel front plates of their new entry-phone systems shining against the dull wet granite, the cheap, drab-painted doors and cheap, ugly uPVC double-glazed windows, grimed and cobwebbed. The cars parked on both sides of the street; an odd assortment of dulled and rusting bangers and other, incongruously smart vehicles - GTIs, mostly - belonging to better-off people who'd temporarily rented or even bought property here, while they worked their stint in the city before being promoted and transferred away. The shops, which were mostly on the right-hand side, were newsagents and small grocers, chippers, takeaways, charity shops, and an assortment of small businesses either on the slide or starting off from cheap premises. These sold fitted kitchens, ran video libraries (one or two of which were Ritz or Azad franchises and were neon-lit), offered expertise in computers and in 'personal finance'. The occasional bare, twigletty tree stood between the district council's occasional, large new, gold-on-black etched, becrested rubbish bins. Large numbers of empty crisp packets lay sodden in the gutters.

They were stopped only briefly at the St. Machar Drive junction before driving on towards Bucksburn. Jamie eyed Sandiland as they passed it, on their right. He'd been offered a place in a flat there by the university accommodation office the year before. The rent had been unbelievable cheap - less than £8 a week over the session, because the holidays were rent free - but he'd been put off by the stories he'd heard about the place and the violence and dealing and packs of wild dogs. That and two people he knew who had lived in the place had had their flats cleaned out by burglars. Students' flats, they'd said, were targeted; students, even the ones living off their grants, were that much better off than the other inhabitants.

He'd still, even though he'd been in Aberdeen three years now, and had studied less than a mile from the place, never set foot in the estate.

Then they drove through Bucksburn. It had never, for him, been anything more than a road.

"So Jamie, you're going to be living on the farm again?" asked George.

He never really had known how to take George. Thinking about it, he'd known the man most of his life, and his manner hadn't really, as far as he could remember, changed at all since the time that he could be sure he had a perceptive and honest memory of him. George had always, to people of his own age, like his father, been open and friendly. He'd always told jokes, ones that were as blue as he'd thought would be taken the right way. He'd always been good at telling them; he had a voice that was good for telling them, even-pitched, even though his accent was a bit too strong to let him mimic others convincingly.

Even when he'd worked in the oil and been sent abroad, they'd been visited by him a couple of times a year, and he and his father mainly had sat with him and talked (except that he'd hardly opened his mouth) for seven or eight hours at a stretch. The conversations had often begun at the dinner table - George had had an uncanny habit of always and unexpectedly arriving just after they'd finished eating, so the visit had always begun with them sitting in the kitchen while his mother put the soup back on and saw what else she could feed him - and had always finished well after supper, well after it had become dark if it was winter, with George eventually forcing himself out into the weather and across the court to his car after having been two or three times persuaded to stay a while longer.

There were some topics that always came up when George and his father met. Most of all they shared the same politics - they were rural working-class Tories. They laughed at the notion of joining a union. They damned almost every employer or manager they'd ever worked for or under as being an incompetent, over-paid and often snobbish nonentity who had no idea of how to improve the work that they themselves spent most of their working lives frustrated in doing less well than they saw was possible. Famous gypes of their own generation, unlucky men notorious for their handlessness, were remembered and destroyed. And then, there were the young.

"What this country needs," his father had said once, "is a year or two with Hitler in charge. By Christ, he'd gar them loup."

"Aye, you're right there Jock." But George looked solemn. His elder brother had been captured at St. Valery and had died in Germany a POW.

"He was a coarse bugger, but some of these young shites hanging about pretending to work could dae with a taste o' his medicine."

There had been a pause, which had given Jamie time to brace himself.

"How would you get rid of him, though?"

The faintest of smiles had crossed George's face. Jamie had the feeling that George had seen how necessary and stupid he'd thought the question to be, and after that night had always had the feeling that George had a bit of time for him. Unlike the old man, who hadn't taken kindly to his interruption.

He still got the feeling that people often thought there wasn't much middle ground with George - that he was either telling jokes, or being extremely serious: earnest, even.

"Man, ye're a cocky shite getting," his father had said, after George had left. There were patterned veins vivid across his face.

"All I did was ask a question."

All the same, he hadn't been surprised at the outburst. He remembered the time when he was younger and had tried to challenge another visitor about something he'd said - something completely inconsequential, about Rolls Royce car engines being the best there were. He and his brothers had enjoyed - separately - the usual preadolescent male fantasies about cars and other mechanical things. What the visitor, an uncle they very rarely saw, had said had clearly (then) been wrong, and had to be challenged. And it was a chance to join in this rite his father practised, of having the kind of conversation he never had with his family.

His father had swung the steel toecap of his boot hard against the sharp edge of his son's shinbone. Jamie would always remember sitting there on the settee as the conversation carried on (almost) as if nothing had happened, too terrified to try and get up and leave, trying not to cry with the pain and humiliation.

"It's not your place tae ask questions about things you know nothing aboot," had said his father, after his visitor left. And then he had picked up the paper, and had read it.

"I said, so Jamie you're going to be living on the farm again," said George, in his most pronounced and half-parodic, enunciative manner. He was bawling, so as to make himself heard above the hammering of the engine without having to turn around to face him.

"Aye."

George looked at him sideways, then at Scott, who was still looking out the window, before shaking his head. "By Christ," he said.

"What are you girning at now?" Scott could hardly be heard, with half his face pressed against the side window. He still had a token hand on his arm.

"Happy chappies you two are not. I had more conversation from my passengers when I drove the bloody hearse."

Scott looked round. There was genuine disgust in George's tone.

"You drove a hearse?"

"Aye, and I had wittier conversationalists than you two in the back when I did."

Jamie couldn't help laughing.

"When was this, like?" asked Scott.

"About two years ago," replied George. There was a pause before he continued, and his voice had returned to normal. "It was just after I chucked the last rig. I needed a job, and I didnae fancy going back to fairm wi the auld man, and that job came up." He sniffed; he sounded almost defensive. "I wanted to stay in the town."

"What was it like?" Scott's face had reddened; his voice was quavering.

"It wasnae a bad job in some ways, actually. I mean the money was poor and it was collar and tie all the time, but there were some characters that worked there - the ones that had stuck it. We didnae have anything else tae dae with the relatives or onything, and I wasna given anything to do with getting the bodies ready either. I mostly just drove and looked after the hearse."

Scott was silently creasing himself, with his forehead braced against the dashboard before him; all Jamie could see was his juddering Levi's jacket back, taut against the hunched shoulders. He wondered (because it was what had instantaneously leapt to his own mind) if Scott was thinking of George, this heavy, often ponderous man, in his dark suit, shouldering a coffin into a kirkyard. Like something out of Laurel and Hardy. And then there was the nervous adolescent hysteria at the concept of death, that he still felt the ripples of within himself. But he thought he could also imagine George's pain at being repeatedly made to witness others' grief. He remembered the quietness with which George had often reminisced about his father, who had died a long death, from cancer, in bedridden agony. He felt this desperate need to keep George's attention away from the sight of this fool who, gasping for air, seemed to be far away from the finish of his hysterics.

"So why did you leave?" Jamie asked.

"Well," George seemed to need to prepare himself for the telling. "Boy I was working wi dropped his end of a coffin we were carrying across the crematorium car park."

Jamie, despite himself, laughed. Scott, struggling for breath, sounded as though he was about to die. He was now down sideways on the seat, his head poised over the handbrake. George himself obviously had to work a little to suppress a smile.

"Coffin split open and some of the body spilled oot oo'er."

"What, an arm?"

"No. Boy had had a post-mortem, and some lazy bugger hadnae stitched him up properly. Or being dropped spoilt some o the stitching, anyway. We were trying to put the coffin on its side so's we could hae a look at the bottom - it was there the thing had split - when one o the boys reached under and felt something on his hand, and we began to smell it."

"Oh, Jesus Christ," said Jamie. Scott, though still laughing, had sat up and was obviously trying to bring himself under control again.

"Aye, I'll never forget yon," said George. There was no relish in his voice at having shocked them. "It was enough to put me back on the rig."

The Birds of Kellie Law

Haworth Hodgkinson

There was no wind over the darkened rolling hills
Scattered with trees and orchards,
Only silence when the voices began.
At first a single call from a distant tree,
Then replies from trees awakening
In different directions,
Until the whole landscape seemed to resound
To the serenely plaintive response
Of these unseen unknown birds.
I sensed no purpose
To this gentle fierce polyphony
Filling the night air,
And yet I could imagine these creatures
Performing the same ceremony
Every night,
Creatures seeming at rest in an existence
Far preferable to my own.
I felt far removed from my daily urban realm,
The calmless routine from which only hours separated me,
And yet I felt no unease at my intrusion.
My inner heart wanted to remain forever,
To surrender to this music of an hundred thousand years,
But ill-learned discipline knew I could not stay.
I knew I had glimpsed some other world
From far beyond my childhood
Which could never be mine,
A world in which I had nor place
Nor meaning.

**BREAKING NEW
GROUND
shortlisted poem**

An excerpt from ...
How Long Does Lonesome Last?
Mary MacCall

CHAPTER ONE

Mary sat in the middle of the "clootie rug", watching her mother tidy up. She didn't know what was the matter with her mum these days, but she always seemed to be in a bad mood. Being only six, Mary didn't understand that big people went through mood swings. All she knew was that no matter what she did, it was wrong. She ran her fingers through the mat which her mum had made a few weeks before, using scraps of material and a funny hook. The mat was the most colourful thing in the hut, and Mary took great pleasure in looking at all the bright colours. The hut that she shared with her mum and dad, three brothers and her sister, was an old Army hut that had been built to house the soldiers during the Second World War. Mary was born the week after the war ended, so was ignorant about it. The place she lived at was called Logie Camp, and consisted of about fifty Nissen huts. They were round huts, covered in corrugated iron. In the summer they were stiflingly hot, but in the winter months they were freezing cold. Mary hated the cold, and was always nearest to the pot bellied stove that stood in the middle of the room.

Beth, Mary's elder sister by two years and nine months, was sitting at the table doing her homework. She was the quieter of the two girls, and was the studious type and very brainy, or so Mary thought. Mary had been going to school since she was four. She used to follow Beth and her eldest brother, Robbie to school every day and, in the end, the teacher let her come into the classroom, with the result that, by the time she was five, she had learned the rudiments of reading and writing. The funny thing was that, now she had to go to school, she hated it.

Robbie, her eldest brother, was ten. She never saw much of him. He was always out playing football, or running with his girdy. He had a mop of black curly hair, and sometimes mum broke the comb trying to get the tangles out. Frank and Abbie were the babies of the family. Frank was four years younger than Mary, and was a beautiful child. He had lovely blonde curly hair, pale blue eyes, and was the frailest of the family. Abbie, the baby, was a year younger than Frank and he too had soft golden curls, and at the moment was learning to walk. Mary loved her two little brothers and was like a little mother to them. Sometimes she got fed up with them though. Especially if she wanted out to play with her own pals but mum made her stay in to watch them. She was, by nature, a tom boy, and was for ever getting into trouble for being too dirty or tearing her clothes, or for chattering on and on, or for singing in her bed at night when everyone else wanted to sleep. She just couldn't stay still for five minutes, and many a clout round the ear she got for back chatting her mum or dad. It seemed to her that Beth never got into any trouble, and Mary thought she was miss goody two shoes.

Although Mary was six, she could have passed for four, she was so tiny. She was the plainest of the children, but always had a twinkle in her eye and an infectious laugh. All in all she was a happy child. Mum was a serious sort of person, and didn't laugh much, but dad was very funny and made Mary laugh a lot. He had been shot in the face during the War by a machine gun and it made him seem sinister to other people, but Mary had never known him otherwise so she didn't give a hoot about it.

Mum asked her to set the table for supper and Mary thought if she saw another plate of porridge, or bowl of brose, she would puke. She didn't know what "poverty" meant; she had never heard the word. She knew that, like everyone else at the camp, they were poor and that they, like her family, had to wear cast-off clothes, and do without lots of things. She knew what ration books were because she had to go to the shop with one and get messages for her mum. She knew what money was because dad took home money every Friday and, maybe once or twice a year, she got a silver three penny piece to buy some sweets. Once, when she had been given her three penny bit, Beth and she were on their way to the shop, when she lost her money in the long grass.

She searched and searched but couldn't find it, so she ran back to the hut and took another one out of her mum's purse. Hell of all hell broke loose when mum caught her in the act. She got the daddy of all hidings that day, but it taught her a sharp and painful lesson. Never steal.

Autumn was nearly over, and the hut was beginning to get cold again.

Dad sometimes found an old lemonade bottle and, at nights, he filled it with hot water and wrapped an old sock round it, and they took it in turns to heat their beds at night. Mum and dad's bed was in the living room. Mary and Beth shared a bedroom and so did the three boys. Beth suffered with terrible chilblains and chapped legs, but Mary only got the chapped legs where her welly boots rubbed at the top. Sometimes it was so cold in the hut that Mary couldn't sleep, and would quietly try and sneak in between her mum and dad. Sometimes it worked and sometimes it didn't. Her dad had kept his old khaki great coat from the War and, when it got really cold, he would spread it on top of their meagre bedding. There were no top sheets on the beds and the two blankets were so prickly it was impossible to cuddle into them. Mum and dad had a lovely woollen blanket on their bed, all knitted with old jumpers and cardigans that no-one could wear.

Once Mary had given away mum's woollen blanket. What happened was, the rag and bone man had arrived at the camp and, as usual, all the children came running to see what was in his old van. Mary ran as fast as her wee legs could carry her and, breathless, she reached the van, just as the driver was opening the doors. Her eyes nearly popped out of her head. A doll, almost as big as herself, was hanging on a bit of string at the side of the van. It was beautiful. It was all made of cloth, even the face, and the hair was a mass of curly wool. It had long dangly legs, and wore blue and white striped leggings. It only had four fingers on each hand but she didn't care. Mary just had to have it. She asked the man what she had to do to get it and he told her to ask her mother for lots of old woollies. Once more, Mary took off like a rocket, and ran to the hut to ask her mum for lots and lots of woollens. Disappointment took her breath away when she discovered that her mum was nowhere to be seen. What could she do? She was terrified that someone else would get the doll, so she grabbed the blanket off her mum's bed - the same blanket that had taken her mother ages to knit - and ran as fast as her legs would carry her back to the van. The blanket was so heavy she could hardly carry it and she tripped over it time and again, but finally she made it. The doll was still there and she pushed the blanket into the man's hands, and asked for the doll. He asked her if her mum knew that she had taken the blanket and, after a moment's hesitation, she said yes. She knew it was bad to tell lies, but she had to have a real doll of her own and, when the doll was safely in her arms, she walked happily back to the hut. She hugged the doll tightly to her breast, and its arms were long enough to go round her neck. It felt so good that she didn't notice the oily musty smell that came from it. She loved it.

Her happiness was short lived, however, for her mum caught her going into the bedroom with the doll clasped tightly to her chest. She asked Mary where she had got the doll and, when Mary told her, she threw a mental fit. She grabbed Mary by the shoulders and dragged her back to the rag and bone man. She demanded her blanket back, snatching the doll from Mary and throwing it into the back of the van. By this time Mary was bawling her head off, but her cries seemed to inflame her mum all the more. When they were back inside the hut, mum gave her the biggest hiding of her young life. She was thrown into her bedroom and lay sobbing in a corner for what seemed like hours. She fell into an exhausted sleep, and it was sleeping in the corner of the room her dad found her when he came home from work. When she woke up, she was sitting on her dad's knee. She looked up into his face. Mary had stopped crying. He gently told her that what she had done was very wrong, and that there were lots of things in this life that we wanted, but sometimes, most times, we didn't get them. He said that he knew she wanted the dolly so bad that she didn't think about what she was doing, but taking the blanket off his and mum's bed meant that he and mum would be cold in bed at night, and Mary wouldn't like that to happen, would she? Mary slowly shook her head, climbed down off her father's knee, and made her way to her bedroom. She went into bed knowing there would be no supper for her that night, and wished with all her heart that she had never set eyes on the blooming doll.

One night, at the end of October, a very cold wintry wind had arisen and, being so near the North Sea, a bitter chilly wind was howling round their hut. Mary woke up, frozen to the bone. She tried snuggling nearer to Beth, who told her in no uncertain terms to stay at her own side of the bed. Mary lay for a while, teeth chattering, and with sore muscles, hunching her limbs trying vainly to get some heat into her wee body. Mary had never had a pair of pyjamas or a nightie, nor had Beth. They both wore very old jumpers or cardigans of mum's to sleep in, but with only two old blankets on their bed, the cold wasn't long in penetrating their bodies. Mary gave up and, trying not to disturb Beth, crawled out of bed, making her way to her parents, who slept in the living room. Hoping they would both be asleep, she cautiously climbed into bed beside them. She held her breath for a moment and, when no voice told her to get back to her own bed, she relaxed. The heat was wonderful, and very soon she began to feel sleepy. She was just about to nod off when she heard her mum say something to her dad. They were talking very quietly so as not to disturb her. As she slowly managed to get the gist of their conversation, a stab of fear went through her. As far as she could make out, her mum was going into hospital, and would be there for at least three weeks, and was worried about how they would all manage without her. Dad was telling her not to worry. They would all be fine and were lucky that two of their neighbours had offered to look after the children. Mary and Beth were to stay with Mrs Fraser, who was a nice lady, and the boys were to stay with Mrs Leslie, who was an old battle-axe. Mary couldn't keep up the pretence of sleep any longer and asked her mum why she had to go to hospital. Mum told her that she was going to get an operation so that she couldn't have any more babies, that five of them were enough to feed and clothe, and that she had to have her womb out, whatever a womb was. Mary woke up next morning crying because she thought her mum had died and, it was such a relief to see her pottering about, that she ran to her mum and hugged her legs. Mary made a promise to herself that she would be a good girl and not do anything bad ever again, as long as her mum was alright. Probably that was why her mum was always in a bad mood, because she was scared, so Mary told her not to be scared, that, when she was in getting her tonsils out everything was fine, and her throat had only been sore for about a week.

The bitter cold weather persisted for about a week but, being in the far north east of Scotland, they had it worse than most. Inside, the hut was almost as cold as outside, and the draught whistled under the door. Dad tried to block it with old rags, and it did help a little, but the floors were as cold as ice: they were made of concrete and had well worn linoleum on top. They all wore ``moggans″, which were just old socks with the tops cut off. Moggans were very slippery on the lino, and many a crack they got when their feet went out beneath them! Dad used to go out at nights and chop down some trees. It was illegal, but with five bairns to keep warm he had no option.

Limmer

Grainne Smith

The horizon wis lined wi black crayon,
The grey clouds lowerin an grim,
I wa'ked by this restless limmer
An I thocht o him.

BREAKING NEW
GROUND
1st prize,
poetry

I thocht on the smell o his jersey,
An the shirt I still sleep in at nicht,
I wait for the voice in the glimmer,
Hame-comin in mornin's caul licht.

Nae body aside me,
Nae warmth ava,
Nae hand at ma breist,
Jist memories tae ca.

I mind on his smile as he ca'd me his quine,
His touch as his eyes said the rest,
Noo sine that bitch his claimed him
It's a caul empty warld tae be faced.

Bit rinnin' aside me a wee lauchin loon
Maks ma hairt loup wi pride an wi pain,
His voice an his smile fair mak me stoon -
He's his faither a ower again.

Three Nasty Fables
from The North Sea Scrolls
Duncan McLean

THE FISH AND THE FIK-MA-FAK

Andsons were fined two hundred quid theday for selling illegal fishcakes. They only had fifteen percent fish in them, and thirtyfive is the minimum you're allowed if you want to call them fishcakes. It'd be okay to have one percent fish and the rest sweepings off the floor if you called them sweepings-off-the-floor-cakes, apparently; it's the name that makes all the difference. That's what the sheriff said. The fishcake-buying public are entitled to better, he said, and gave Jimmy Andson two weeks to pay. Two hundred quid in two weeks? No bother to the likes of him. He could've paid that much in two seconds, though he didn't. Ken when he'll pay? After one week, six days, twentythree hours and fiftynine minutes. And some seconds.

I wasn't surprised when I heard the news - Jimmy's always been a devious bugger. Like his name, that wasn't come about with honesty. (I can say that here, he won't take it to his face.) Really he's Jimmy Anderson; that's what he was born. But cause he fell out with his brother so bad, he decided he'd change it, he'd change his identity. Just so everybody would ken for sure where he began and his brother ended. So he dropped a couple letters and became Andson.

And look at the state of things now! His lad, David, he's fourteen, and he wants to go into the business - he gets on better with fish than with folk, everybody kens. But what's Jimmy going to paint up over his shop door? Andson And Son? The town'll be a laughing stock. What a fucking fik-ma-fak!

THE BULL AND THE BRAT

There was this farmer, a crofter you would call him, by the name of Willie Johnson. All he had was two one-acre fields out the front of his house. But that was alright, for he only had one cow. Now Willie had a friend up the hill, and his friend was called Jack Noble. Jack had a bull by the name of Randy, a fine big beast, and that was no problem at all either, till one day Jack came down the hill with Randy on a chain and said, Willie, I'm away on holiday, will you look after my bull for me?

I've only got two fields, said Willie.

Well, put your cow in one and Randy in the other, said Jack.

That'll no work, said Willie. You ken what Randy's like. It'd take more than a rickety fence to stop him: once he gets the sight of a bonnie cow's arse, it'd take the Great Wall of China to keep him in.

You're right, said Jack, so here's what we'll do: we'll brat her. Away and get an old sheet off Williamina.

Willie shakes his head, but off he goes and gets an old white sheet off his wife. Now what? he says.

Now, says Jack, we tie this sheet over your cow's tail, hiding the good looking end of her from Randy, and letting me leave him with everybody's honour protected.

So that's just what they did. They tied the sheet over the tail of Willie's cow and then they lead Randy into the park next door, and he never even looked at her. And off drove Jack for his weekend in Aberdeen. Willie was a bit nervous, but the plan seemed to be working, so he went to bed as usual.

All through the night he had terrible dreams of bulls rutting and bellowing, of Randy smashing down great walls to reach his heart's desire. He woke up at dawn, sweating, and nudged Williamina awake.

Wife, wife, said Willie. I'm feart to look: go over to the window and tell me, is she alright?

Is who alright? said Williamina.

Samantha, said Willie, My cow with the sheet tied over her tail.

So Williamina bauchles to the window, looks out, and grunts. There's no cow with a sheet tied over her tail there, she says.

What! shouts Willie, sitting bolt upright, No cow with a sheet over its tail?

No, says Williamina, But there is one with a hankie up its cunt.

THE TOURISTS AND THE CHICKENS

The tourists got to sleep despite the uproar in the bar downstairs. Then the woman woke up. She had a funny feeling. Plus there was light coming in from the corridor, when the door should've been shut. She elbowed her man.

Julian! Wake up!

Eh? What is it?

I've a funny feeling.

Eh?

It feels like somebody's kissing my feet.

Well put on the light.

It's on your bloody side!

Julian groped about and found the lamp and switched it on. A big buldery guy in a boilersuit was kneeling at the bottom of the bed, his head down behind the woman's feet and the lump of the folded-back quilt.

He's licking my toes! she cried.

Julian roared, and the big guy looked up and yelled, Jeggseggs Chreggst! Feggck megg! Then he fell over backwards and started crawling away out of the room.

Call the manager, said the woman.

Where's the phone? said the guy.

There isn't one.

Jesus Christ, what kind of place....

Get him! she screamed.

Julian jumped out of bed and ran to the door, then came back in for his dressing gown before rushing off again. By that time the guy in the boilersuit was long gone.

Next morning, Sid the manager was in a right stoosh, haring about telling everybody that his reputation was ruined unless the pervert was caught.

But that wasn't a pervert, said Jimmy Andson. That was...

Just some daft drunk laddie, I came in, and frowned at Jimmy the gowk.

Sid banged out of the shop and went off tae be outraged all over the village.

Jimmy turned to me. That sounds awful like Feathery Willie from the poultry farm, he said.

Of course it was bloody Feathery Willie! I said. Who else speaks that daft eggy language?

Willie laughed. Him and his fucking chickens! he said. They'll get him into trouble some day.

He's alright as long as he sticks to the chickens, I said. It's when he starts mixing it with the human race that disaster strikes. Now give me my fucking fishcakes.

For Evelyn Glennie

Bill Sluyter

As a tepid sun
Cast long shadows
I gently wiped
The sleep from
Your eyes with
Soft-headed mallets.
It was as if
You had marimbad
Away the darkness,
And drummed in
The advance of morning.

There Was This Man

Bill Sluyter

There was this man.....

A pianist he was.
Spent his life trying
To bend notes on his piano.

He knew it couldn't
Be done.

Yet still he tried,
His torso arched,
Fingers splayed and coaxing.

It was akin to
Loving her.

You knew it couldn't
Be done.

A Fisherboy's Training
from the novel 'The Golden Belger'
Robert Stephen

But a fat lot of welfare was there in Cotton Toon in 1912, so Weelum said to Lizzy, "Stick to the beuks, dother."

Billy wisna interested and before fourteen years had quit school as a bad job and could whup a ripper heuk so techt on the sneed that ye couldna furl it in the knot. He rowed with his faader in the Gracious at the Gowan Hole and vrocht harder for his breid than ony Roman slave.

Lizzy had asked Billy aboot salvation by 'works' or by Brethren 'grace' and he said, "A fat lot of grace there wis in the Gracious." And he said, "You'll hae to look in the kest up in the laft in the Brethren beuks."

Billy wisna interested in heid work unless it wis to do with herrin or hoddecks.

Weelum wis as hard as iron in training Billy. A sailin bate demands crew that are deft and powerful in all their workings of the sails and nets and lines. There wis nae easy way in the vrocht of the auld bates, bonny as the great sail fleet wis, passing the Cotton Shore in a herring-filled morning.

Behold upon the hempen tackle, ship-boys hauling;
Hear the steady splash of the sharp bows through the deep sea;
Behold the threaden sails, borne with the invisible and creeping wind,
draw the big bates through the furrow'd sea, breasting the lofty surge.
O! do but think, you stand upon the shore, and behold a city on the
inconstant billows dancing;
For so appears this fleet majestical.

But on the lovely bates, the working needs of the ships governed the training rather than the inclinations of the faaders' souls, so that their hearts were hardened to create tough seamen oot of raw boys and their fresh, smooth facies and minds still tuned in to play, although they had been helping row the auld men's partan yoles since bairnies struggling in their bare feeties with bougies to drav the yolies up and doon the shores.

Billy's lugs had been derled mair than eneuch and he had been ca'ed skite across the ballast with a boat-hook across his back. His aulder cousins, Weelum and Jimmy, objected and threatened his faader that they widna drav his yole again nor sail in the herrin bate wi' him on board!

So Weelum had said, "A' recht, you look after him yersels."

And they did because they had been trained by Lizzy's faader themsels in the ways of fisher boys who had to haul and spew and spew and haul when the bates lifted and rolled, and the masts creaked across the sweltering seas.

So Billy gave up the beuks, "For in much study is a weariness of the flesh and in making mony beuks there is no end." But with great knowledge comes great responsibility spoke the Great Preacher, "For that servant, which KNEW his Lord's wull and prepared not himsel, neither did accordin to His wull, shall be beaten with many stripes."

So it wis that Weelum laid on the stripes on Billy. Lizzy shuddered at the welts across his young face and she couldna resign or square the hardness of the training to the rigour of the fisherman's lot and she held a theerup against her faader for his cruel and crabbit scowpins.

Lizzy thocht, naethin could justify this roch dreelin; nae even the Lord's wull. But the Beuks does say, "To whom men have committed much, of him will they ask the more." And on a sailin bate, the very maximum of human endurance and alertness and skill is asked for and the task master is the great roarin tempest and the sye will aye tame fools.

It may be a' recht for a learned preacher full of beuks to, "Lay doon into the sides of the ship and gyang fast asleep" whiles the crew struggled on deck and "Cried every man to his own god and worked to save the ship from being broken by the mighty tempest and the great wind sent into the sea". But then, the sailors threw the preacher into the sea and a great fish swallowed HIM!

So Billy avoided the beuks and took the hard vrocht and the roch treatment on his boyish chin. He wisna gyan to be like him that the phal swallit! But the same faader said, "Stick en to the learnin Lizzy, for that is the pathway awa from the creel and the poverty that shackles you to the back-breakin slavery imposed by the fish and the yoles; and awa frae the unendin fish diet, day in and day oot a' your life lang." For it's saat herrin and kippers and hairy-wully; speldins steepit in haet water afore the fire; boiled cod and cod heid soup; fried hoddeck and fried herrin; smokit fyshe and January rans from the spawnin codlins.

Lizzy likit best the half-blavin keilin roasted on the bronner wi' their juices sizzlin and dreepin into the peat firie. You jist got awfa fed up and mangit for a bitty beef you couldna afford except on Sundays in good times.

Wis the fishing aye gyan to be sae hard? You couldna a' be lawyers and doctors and teachers.

A doctor body earned twenty pounds a week against a tradesman's one powin for a week's chavin. It's money that gives you the fine claese and hooses and grone things and a full belly and respectability.

Maybe Billy wid get a berth aboard uncle Jocky's and Bob's new steam drifter, the Gowan Lea, being built soon.

Compared to the open sailin bates, the drifters were paradise with their tall funnels rickin and their ten knots speed fitiver the widder, ween or calm. They worked mair nets and carried ten of a crew; a driver and fireman, mair than the sailin bates, so there wid be berths for Billy in much safer ships. But the auld fishermen said that they were too expensive, making money for the coal-man and the wind that filled the bates' sails was free from the hand of God.

They said that greater poverty than ever would come with the steam age.

So that wis the Lizzie of the airs and graces of the grone folk and the learned class. But the other Lizzie was bent over, to the slope of the rack and the creel on her back at the Gowan Hole and the saat wind lifting her skirt up and across her smooth, slender legs, white as snow against the dark, rough-spun cloth.

And the young fisher lads standing on the skaelies were grinning and gazing at her all sonsy and fresh and firm of face and body as supple as a green wun by the riverside.

She balanced her laden wecht on her bare feet, curled ower the grey pebbles and she smiled back to the blue gangees and caught an eye here and there and she wis glad to be a bonny fisher lassie, clean-blavin by the cauld oot-wins sharp as knives. And she wis pleased they liked the look of her.

But the fishy smell of their fear-not bricks, streaked white with dried saat; and their unwashed working hands specked with fish scales would disgust the learned side of her and force her heid back amang the musty beuks and awa to ancient Gaul with Caesar ridding the Celtic druids of the greedy, German warrior tribes and driving the Huns back across the Rhine. Victorious Caesar in his gold helmet and quick legal mind and musical tongue braigin, ˈVeni, vidi, vici!ˈ wis a far cry from the Cotton fisher boys descended from the once proud Picts of whom he couldna say, ˈI came and saw and conqueredˈ. And she thocht, Och Caesar's jist an orra Mediterranean mannie lang deid. She peeped at the lads' eyes upon her and saw the pain of longing, pining behind the young, sea-beaten faces.

Spring wis coming and the nechts were receding from the strengthening lecht of the sun and, this day, Lizzy stumbled and fell forward on the rack and the creel lurched and doon she went. The lads, standing on the rocks lached.

But one came forward and picked up the creel and held it high and grasped her arm to steady her.

She raised her heid and brushed her burnished umber hair from her brow with her arm and looked at Jeemse, keen and quick of thought, his fair young face smiling at her through grey eyes narrowed to hide his shyness, and he said, ˈAre you a' recht?ˈ

She nodded and heard her voice, ˈWhy are you nae ower there lachin like the rest?ˈ

A red tinge flushed below his eyes but the manly dignity of the ancient Pict of old Tershinnity was in him and he showed not his feelings in his face but in his breast and his spasmodic breathin showed what was there. He had a long-time dream of a Lily amang thorns and fancy was now engendered before his eyes, but he couldna tell her that; so he mocked her, ˈWhy are YOU nae greetin wi your fall?ˈ

She lached full and wide, her lips open and dark eyes gazing at him straight and seein the dream behind his grey eyes.

She felt strange and him standing there holding the creel like a shield and tall as a tree and she knew then he was the shade for this fair Lily, but she said nothing and peeked throw her hair at his expression switherin fit to say next.

He said, "Here!" Turning her back to him, he lifted the fettle ower her blaze of copper red tresses and she took the wecht of the creel of fish. But as she grasped the strap, his hand, hardened with the rowing, touched her fingers and for a second they both kent each ither's dreams.

Lizzy swung easily along the fit o' toon. White wisps of clouds laughed across the sky from the Belger Pint o' Heid and her lungs dragged in the saat-laden Northerly breeze and so to dress the fish and to the scrubbing tub. Her great locks, flowing like Hymen veil down to her slender waist were in the way so she swept them up and knotted them back from her face. And ower the tub, a Brethren girl, now grasped a codlin upon the board and swiftly the blade swung with skill from the shoulder and separated fish from bone.

But doon there at the Gowan Hole, she had crossed to the golden time that she searched for in the Laws of Nature and in the histories of other golden ages when men did not compete for land or fish and the catch wis shared through the tribe and there were no fences across property nor Pharisee taboos across the love of a quine for her lad; nor any hidden places of shame - all innocent afore the Fatal Tree.

She kent that Caledonia's dour and bleak and wintry skies wid niver again be pressin doon so painfully upon the lonely times of her soul, for golden springtime had entered sparkling in a vernal stream through her veins and spreitly heart. So she sang to hersel leanin ower the tub of cod, the sangie from the great pastoral bard:

It was a lover and his lass,
With a hey, and a ho, and a hey nonino,
That o'er the green corn-field did pass,
In the spring time, the only pretty ring time,
When birds do sing, hey ding a ding, ding;
Sweet lovers love the spring.

So she sang in the wash-hoose below the meeting hall laftie, this un-Brethren hymnie, but Lizzie kent that a fisher lad's heart had entered into her bosom.

The Pie Ring
Brian Adams

Mobil

joint winner of
1994 MOBIL
SCOTTISH
PLAYWRIGHTS'
COMPETITION

The play is set in the sixties and takes place at the pastry table of a large bakery in Aberdeen - the Northern Co-operative Society, which was later called NORCO and which is now defunct.

The centrepiece of the set is a large work table. The upstage entrances require space for wheeled racks and a barrow to move on and off freely. There is a drinking well DL, a clock on the wall and a gas ring R. The fresh goods required as props should present no difficulties. The materials used do not all have to be real pastry and with a little ingenuity the use of real mince will be avoided!

No baking skills are required. The pie mince is runny and is spooned into the pie cases. Bridie mince is thicker and the dropping of it onto the pastry cases is quite a skill, but in the play it is done inexpertly by an apprentice doing it for the first time. Anybody can put lids on pies and line flan tins.

The characters:

Eddie	Ovensman, mid 40s
Kenny	Doughman, mid 40s
Alex Rennie	Foreman, 40-60
Bill Smith	Pastryman, late 40s
Charlie	Tablehand, 60s
Sam Murry	Tablehand, Union Branch Secretary, Town Cllr, 40-60
Allan	2nd year apprentice, about 17
Alex Thompson	Bakery Manager, mid 50s

Kenny and Alex Thompson may be played by the same actor. All have strong Aberdeen City accents except possibly Thompson who can hail from anywhere in Scotland and Charlie who is "country", Aberdeenshire style. Why not send the audience home with a freshly baked scotch pie (curry flavoured)?

ACT 1

Scene 1

4.00am Friday

THE SET IS IN DARKNESS. "TELSTAR" IS PLAYED. WHEN THE MUSIC STOPS A HEAVY SLIDING DOOR BEING OPENED IS HEARD AND THE LIGHTS FLICKER ON TO FLOURESCENT BRIGHTNESS. FOOTSTEPS ARE HEARD APPROACHING AND WORDLESSLY EDDIE PETRIE AND KENNY SIM ENTER UR. EDDIE CARRIES STRAIGHT ON AND OFF UL TOWARDS THE OVENS. KENNIE GOES TO THE DESK AND READS AN ORDER SHEET FOR A MOMENT. HE LOOKS AT A RACK BESIDE THE DESK WHICH CONTAINS SEVERAL PANS OF CURRANT LOAVES COVERED WITH TISSUE PAPER AND, LOOKING IN THE DIRECTION OF THE OVENS TO CHECK THAT HE IS UNSEEN, HE TAKES A LOAF FROM THE CENTRE OF A PAN AND STUFFS IT INSIDE HIS APRON BIB AND EXITS UR WITH THE ORDER SHEET IN HIS HAND

EDDIE ENTERS UL AND EXITS UR TO APPEAR A FEW SECONDS LATER PUSHING A CART LOADED WITH COKE. HE STOPS UR AND, LOOKING IN THE DIRECTION OF THE MIXERS TO CHECK THAT HE IS UNSEEN, HE ALSO TAKES A LOAF FROM THE CENTRE OF THE PAN AND HIDES IT IN HIS APRON BIB. HE MOVES BACK TO HIS CART AND CARRIES ON TO EXIT UL.

THE WHINE OF A MIXING MACHINE MOTOR STARTING UP SETTLES TO A LOW GRINDING RHYTHM. THIS IS REPEATED AND THE SOUND OF TWO MACHINES CONTINUES.

KENNY ENTERS UR LOOKING AROUND AND MUTTERING ANGRILY TO HIMSELF

KENNY (CALLING IN THE DIRECTION OF THE OVENS) Eddie, are my yeast tins doon 'ere?

EDDIE (OFF) Dinna see 'em. Hud on 'till I look.. Aye, th're in the sink.

KENNY 'At lazy bugger o' a loon. Ess is gettin' tae be a habbit wi' 'im. (He exits UL)

THE SOUND OF CLATTERING TINS AND WATER BEING RUSHED OUT OF A TAP IS HEARD OFF. PRESENTLY KENNY RETURNS UL CARRYING THREE LARGE CANS IN EACH HAND AND CROSSES TO EXIT UR WHERE MORE CLATTERING IS HEARD OFF. HE REPEATS THE PROCEDURE AND EXITS WITH ANOTHER SIX CANS HE HAS COLLECTED.

EDDIE ENTERS UL CARRYING A KETTLE WHICH HE PLACES ON THE GAS RING. HE REACHES UNDER THE TABLE AND TAKES OUT SOME TEA THINGS CONTAINED IN A TIN CAN. HE LIGHTS THE GAS AND PUTS SUGAR IN BOTH CUPS AND, LIGHTING UP THE REMAINDER OF A CIGARETTE, HE SMOKES WHILE HE WAITS FOR THE WATER TO BOIL, GIVING A HUGE YAWN AS HE DOES SO.

KENNIE ENTERS UR AND JOINS EDDIE. THE KETTLE BOILS.

KENNY (AS EDDIE REACHES OUT TO PUT OUT THE GAS) Leave on the gas, Eddie, it's cauld in here this mornin'.

EDDIE Aye, it's nippy a' right. Felt it fin I got up. Might rain ana'.

KENNY I think you should start an 'oor afore me an' hae yer ovens warmin' the place up.

EDDIE Christ, Eddie, a fowr start's bad enough. An' a lang Friday in front o's wi' the five day wik startin'.

KENNY It's been a lang time comin' 'at. Fa wid 'ive thocht it, a five day wik for bakers, it's hard tae credit it.

EDDIE (POURING OUT THEIR TEA AND SITTING DOWN ON A DRUM) Aye, an' a' that wis needit wis the auld storeroom turned inti a freezer. We could hiv hid a five day wik twinty year ago!

KENNY Mine, I'm nae happy wi' the frozen stuff thiv bin tryin' oot. I wid say the pastry's a bit o' a disaster. Fit did ye think o' that stuff last Friday?

EDDIE Aboot half as bad again as it usually is. But 'at's nae my problem. I'm jist peyed tae fire the stuff Kenny, nae tae worry aboot whether it's shite or no.

THEY FALL SILENT AND DRINK THEIR TEA. EDDIE GIVES ANOTHER GREAT YAWN.

KENNY Yer like a half shut knife min. Are ye gettin' yer sleep?

EDDIE I could use mair o't right enough

KENNY Yer aye workin' ahin' the bar at the Stag?

EDDIE Aye, an' mair. Ye fuckin' hivtae. The extra for startin' early in here isna the answer tae my fuckin'... (THE SENTENCE FADES AWAY AND THERE IS A SILENCE) ...S o at's yer tins nae washed again?

KENNY Oh aye, thon loon jist pleases himsel'. Thir supposed tae be washed and stacked ready for me in the mornin'. At's the doughs ten minutes late again because I've hid tae ging and rake for the tins. Bloody loon.

EDDIE Oh yer wastin' yer time wi' 'at een. (HE YAWNS AGAIN AND SUDDENLY GETS TO HIS FEET) Jesus! I'd better get yokit afore a fa' asleep.

KENNY MAKES NO MOVE TO RISE BUT THEY ARE BOTH GALVANISED INTO ACTION AT THE SOUND OF SOMEONE APPROACHING. KENNY TURNS OFF THE GAS AND QUICKLY PUTS AWAY THE TEA THINGS AS EDDIE STUBS OUT HIS CIGARETTE ON HIS SHOE AND BRUSHES THE FLOOR WITH HIS FOOT TO DISPERSE ANY SIGNS OF IT. HE DROPS THE STUB INTO HIS APRON BIB AND WAVES THE AIR TO DISPERSE THE SMOKE.

KENNY (LOOKING OFF UR) It's Alex, Fit's he deein in this early?

EDDIE EXITS DL, AS ALEX RENNIE ENTERS UR.

KENNY Aye, aye, Alex, yer sharp this mornin' though?

ALEX Fit like, Eddie. Nae hairm in bein' early the day I think. (LOOKING IN THE DIRECTION OF THE OVENS)

(ALEX SMELLS THE CIGARETTE SMOKE BUT SAYS NOTHING AND MOVES TO THE DESK)

KENNY Alex, I'm fed up o' that Allan. At's me hae'en tae hunt the tins doon again afore I can get a start. Dinna blame me if the doughs are late. He's jist pleasin' himsel. He's needin' a kick in the erse at's fit he's needin'.

ALEX Right, a'll kick his erse.

KENNY TURNS TO LEAVE.

ALEX cont. Like Thompson'll kick the arse o' oanibidy I catch smokin' in the bakehoose right oot the bloody door.

KENNY (STOPPING AND TURNING) Nae me, Alex. Ye winna catch me smokin'.

ALEX Aye, okay.   A'll spik tae the loon.

KENNY EXITS AND ALEX STANDS AT THE DESK AND LIFTS OUT A CLIPBOARD WITH ORDER SHEETS ATTACHED AND READS THEM. AFTER A MOMENT THE PHONE RINGS AND HE CASUALLY PICKS IT UP.

ALEX Sma'breed (HE LISTENS FOR TWO SECONDS AND BECOMES ALERT) Foo lang's he been in? (HE LISTENS AGAIN) Thanks Walter. (HE PUTS THE PHONE DOWN AND SNIFFS THE TOBACCO SMOKE AGAIN) Christ!

HE WAVES THE CLIPBOARD IN THE AIR AS EDDIE ENTERS UL AND MAKES TO CROSS R.

ALEX cont. Thomson's in. Fit will I tell 'im fin he asks fa's bin smokin' in here?

EDDIE (AS HE EXITS UR) Tell 'im oanay fuckin' thing ye like, Alex .

ALEX SHAKES HIS HEAD AND TURNS BACK TO THE DESK.

END OF SCENE.

THE SOUND OF THE MIXERS IN THE BACKGROUND IS RAISED TO A LOUD RUMBLE AND THE LIGHTS DIM.

ACT 1

Scene 2   6.00pm

THE MIXING MACHINE SOUND RETURNS TO A LOW RHYTHM IN THE BACKGROUND AND THE LIGHTS RETURN TO FULL.
DURING THE SCENE CHANGE ALEX REMAINED AT THE DESK. HE TAKES OUT A SMALL ORDER FROM INSIDE THE DESK AND, SLIPPING THE CARBON PAPER ONTO A FRESH PAGE, HE WRITES INTO IT. HE GLANCES UP AT THE CLOCK AND A FEW SECONDS LATER A BELL RINGS. AFTER A MOMENT HE EXITS DR.

PRESENTLY THE APPROACH OF THE MAIN SHIFT IS HEARD AND BILL, SAM AND CHARLIE ENTER UR. BILL CROSSES TO THE DESK AND STUDIES THE ORDER SHEETS, THEN CROSSES TO THE FRONT OF THE TABLE TO TAKE OUT A BASIN FROM THE RACK UNDERNEATH AND EXITS DR. CHARLIE LIFTS THE COVERS FROM THE TABLE AND THEN WHEELS THE RACK OF FLAN TINS OVER TO THE TABLE AND STACKS THE PANS ON TO THE TABLE. KENNY ENTERS CARRYING A BOARD WITH PIE LIDS AND THE LININGS FOR FLAN CASES.

KENNY Nine flans. Fifteen lids.

SAM LIFTS OUT A BASIN AND GOES TO THE STEEL BARREL R AND STARTS TO TRANSFER THE APPLES WHICH HAVE BEEN SOAKING OVERNIGHT INTO THE MIXING BASIN.

SAM Brrr. (AS HE DIPS INTO THE BARREL UP TO HIS ELBOWS)

CHARLIE The aipples warm enough for ye Sam?

SAM It's that time o' year a' richt, Charlie. Brrr. (HE CONTINUES TO LIFT OUT THE APPLES) Time to start puttin' them down beside the ovens overnight, I think. (HE EXITS DL WITH THE APPLES)

BILL RETURNS WITH THE MINCE AND PUTS IT ON THE SIDE TABLE.

CHARLIE (NODDING TO THE BARREL) Cooncillor Murry's feelin' the cauld.

BILL Weel 'at's easy enough sorted, we'll pit them doon the ovens tae soak. He's nae moanin' aboot it is he?

CHARLIE No, he wis jist sayin',

CHARLIE AND KENNY START TO LINE THE FLAN TINS.

KENNY Thompson's in. Been in since four this mornin'. Sai's Alex,

BILL They'll be crappin' themsel's aboot the morn. I dinna see the panic. Near athin's in the freezers. It's jist needin' tae be teemed oot the morn's mornin' and fired.

BILL LOOKS AROUND AND LIFTS A CELLOPHANE PACKAGE OF ABOUT FIVE POUNDS OF MINCE OUT OF THE BASIN CONTAINING A LARGE QUANTITY OF MINCE AND STARTS TO MIX IT IN A SMALLER BOWL.

CHARLIE (REFERRING TO THE MINCE BEING MIXED) Dis the five day wik mean that wir gan' tae hae tae freeze the specials an'a'.

BILL (AS HE ADDS SEASONING AND SALT) No

chance. Wir nae freezin' 'em. Some standards in this place will continue tae be maintained. The customers wid kick up fuck.

THEY LAUGH AGAIN BUT STOP WHEN SAM ENTERS DL AND JOINS THE TABLE GROUP. BILL PLACES THE BOWL OF MINCE UNDER THE TABLE. EDDIE ENTERS UL WHEELING A RACK OF CHELSEA BUNS.

EDDIE Far's Allan. His fuckin' stuff's in the road. He's supposed tae come tae the ovens for his stuff as he kens fuckin' fine.

BILL He's nae in, Eddie.

CHARLIE Watch ess, he'll slide in here in a minute hopin' that Alex hisni' missed 'im yet. He hisni' been takin' weel tae the hoors o' late.

KENNY Neen o's like the hoors, Charlie, he should try a four o'clock start an' see how he likes 'at.

BILL Aye, tell's ess, Sam. Fit wye is Kenny and me still jist gettin' sweeties for an early start fin it's double time a' roon for abdy on Seterdis now.

BILL Weel it's nae worth it 'ats a' that I can say. The union should be deein' mair. A four start's a real bastard, Sam. It's worse than night shift - its nae one thing or the ither.

SAM I ken that. Eddie, but the rate we got for ye is the best you'll get.

BILL Aye, weel...there's somethin' else. (HE NODS WITH HIS HEAD TOWARDS THE DESK) Doon here a minute. (THEY MOVE DOWN) Alex Rennie came in here ess mornin' an' accused me o' smokin' in the bakehoose.

SAM So fit's his evidence?

BILL Neen. So I'm nae gan tae be

accused o' smokin' by him or oanibidy.

SAM Are you makin' an offical complaint? Do you want me to take it up wi' Thompson?

BILL No, but he should be telt tae watch his mooth, 'ats a', or I will tak it futher.

SAM (BLANDLY) Okay, Eddie.

ALEX ENTERS UL AND SEE THE TWO IN CONVERSATION AND MOVES TOWARDS THEM. BILL SEES HIM AND EXITS DL. ALEX JOINS SAM.

ALEX Oanything in 'at conversation for me, Sam?

SAM He's saying you falsely accused him of smokin' in the bakehoose. But he's nae takin' it further.

ALEX I bet he's nae. If he thinks he's bein' victimised or oanythin', you jist tell him tae tak' it tae Thompson. Or if ye wint ti be o' some good till 'im, tell 'im tae stop smoking in the bakehoose.

SAM Steady now, Alex, ye canna...

ALEX ... I cann fit? Canna let him ken that I'm nae feel? He wis smokin' a' richt. Dinna tell me how tae gaffer, Sam. I'm in the union ana' mind.

SAM Fair enough, Alex. I'll be awa at twelve the day.

ALEX Nae bother. (JOKINGLY) Fa is't the day, Sam? The Pope?

SAM No, nithin' like that. A meetin' wi' Thompson first then a council sub-committee in the aefterneen, this ile thing in the north sea's startin' ti look up. Oanywye, thanks Alex. (HE REJOINS THE TABLE GROUP. ALEX GOES OFF DL)

CHARLIE (WHO, LIKE THE OTHERS, OBSERVED THE EXCHANGE) Fit did the Queen hae tae say tae ye yisterday

then, Sam? She seemed tae be natterin' awa tae ye quite the thing on TV.

BILL Maybe askin' ye tae tak' somethin' up wi' the union, wis she?

SAM Na, na. Bill, we're nae that freenlie. I'm just another toon cooncillor oot o' the hunners, I think.

BILL So fit did she say?

CHARLIE (WITH MOCK POSH ACCENT) "Nice o' ye tae tak the afterneen aff yer work tae meet me an' Phil aff the boat. Foo's the co-opie boys aye doin'?....

BILL (ALSO WITH MOCK POSH VOICE) ... is Bill still in charge o' the pies?"

SAM Na, na, na.

CHARLIE So tell's 'en. Fit did she say?

SAM (A BIT UNCOMFORTABLY) Well, she said that the tugs were lookin' nice.

CHARLIE Fit?, the tugs were lookin' nice! You mean ye shut doon Union Street, pint the harbour fae top tae fit, you and the rest o' the council tak' the day aff yer work tae line up like a shortbreed on a pan tae meet the Queen aff her boat an' a' she can spik aboot is foo bonny the tugs are. 'At's nae worth washin' yer face for, min.

BILL I tak' it the tugs had been ge'en a lick o' pint for the occasion.

SAM I think that must have been it. She'd jist noticed that they had been smartened up and said so.

CHARLIE Weel, weel, I niver.

THE TABLE FALLS SILENT FOR A MOMENT.

CHARLIE cont. So fit did you say back till 'er?

SAM Nae much. I just said...

CHARLIE ..."'At's nithin', yer majesty, ye should see the Co-opie coal boat".

SAM Na, a' that I said was that they must have gaen them a lick o' pint.

THE TABLE FALLS SILENT FOR A MOMENT AS THEY TAKE THIS IN.

CHARLIE Weel, sparklin' repartee eh? That wid huv set her back on her high heels. (THEY ALL LAUGH) I wonner she didna fa' back intae Blaikies Quay at 'at een!

BILL Nae like you tae be stuck for somethin' tae say, Sam

SAM (LAUGHING WITH THE REST) Aye, weel, newsin' wi' Queens is obviously nae a strength o' mine.

SAM IS SAVED BY THE ENTRANCE OF ALEX DL.

ALEX (NOTICING THE CHELSEA BUN RACK) Far's Allan?

THE MEN ARE NON-COMITTAL AND CONCENTRATE ON THEIR WORK.

ALEX cont. Late! Fit a loon 'at is. 'At's ivry day 'ess wik.

BILL (POINTING TO THE CURRANT LOAVES) Fit's 'ess loafs deein' here, Alex.

ALEX Thompson's wintin' them iced wi' the chelsea buns. Somethin' new he's tryin'. But thir nae gan tae get iced in a hurry if thiv tae wait for 'at dozy bugger tae get oot o' his bed. Kenny, warm up some icin' an' get started on them.

KENNY Oh c'mon, Alex. At's nae my job.

ALEX It's oan'bdys job, Kenny. Yer doughs are deen so ye can ice loaffs for Godsake. The chelsea buns ana'. He's needin' the loaffs iced pink same's the buns. Go'an then, thi'll be screamin' for them soon. (HE EXITS UR)

KENNY EXITS UR WITH THE RACK AND RETURNS TO COLLECT THE TWO PANS OF CURRANT LOAVES. HE RETURNS AGAIN TO COLLECT A POT FROM UNDER THE TABLE AND GOES OFF DR WITH IT.

THEY FINISH THE FLANS AND SAM TAKES THE RACK OFF UL TO THE OVENS. THE OTHERS START PREPARING TO FILL AND TOP THE PIE CASES.

BILL At's made Kenny's day.

CHARLIE Has he deen the buns afore?

BILL I dinna think so.

CHARLIE A first time for athin', eh?

KENNY ENTERS DR AND GOES TO THE RING TO HEAT UP THE FONDANT.

KENNY At bloody loon should be oot the door.

CHARLIE His Thompson been up again?

BILL Hinna seen'im.

CHARLIE Er's maybe somethin' up ye know. The last time he wis in that early wis tae catch thon feel fae the hotplate pittin' a box o' currants intae the back o' his car. Fit wis his name again? ... Simpson, Ally Simpson.

KENNY I canna min' 'im.

BILL He wisna here lang. He wis jit a crook thon boy. I used tae work wi' 'im fin I did night shift on the hot plate. He'd turn his pancakes an' the next thing, fin' the gaffer's awa tae his break, he's oot the back door wi' a box o' butter or something an' be back tae lift his pancakes afore they burned. I nivver saw oanythin' sae fast.

CHARLIE Mine he drove thon great hoor o' a Citreon. Ye could see how. He wis sellin' the stuff someplace. Thompson wis wised up an' waitin' for him that mornin'...

CHARLIE STOPS SUDDENLY WHEN HE SEES THAT KENNY HAS PUT TOO MUCH COLOUR IN THE ICING AND SILENTLY POINTS THIS OUT TO THE REST.

BILL Hiv ye enough colour in 'ere dae ye think, Kenny?

GRAHAM Fit's wrang wi't.

BILL It's jist that fin Alex said pink I think it wis mair his curtains than Christine Keeler's dra'rs that he hid in mind.

KENNY 'Ers nithin' wrang wi't. (HE EXITS UR)

SAM Christine Keeler disna wear dra'ers.

CHARLIE Dis she nae noo? Weel if she did, ye widna need sunglasses tae tak' them aff like yer gan tae need sunglasses tae eat the co-opie's chelsea buns!

BILL (LOOKING OFF UR) Oh, look at the state o' this.

ALLAN ENTERS UL AND GOES DIRECTLY TO WORK AT THE TABLE, NERVOUSLY LOOKING AROUND TO SEE IF ALEX IS PRESENT.

BILL He wis lookin' for ye.

ALLAN Fuck. I slept in.

CHARLIE G'wa.

ALLAN Aye. (REALISING THAT HE IS BEING MADE FUN OF) Fuck off! (HE DARTS OFF UL)

SAM Far's he awa' till?

BILL (LAUGHING AND LOOKING OFF) He's awa lookin' for his buns.

SAM He canna rise 'at loon. I think he must be in amongst the weemin.

BILL He's playin' in a band as weel, 'at disni' ging wi' six o'clock starts.

CHARLIE Aye bit yir job's ti' come first, Bill. You keep busy wi' your band an' yir golf an' a' the rest o't but ye still get inti yir work.

BILL A' the loons ging through this. Dae ye nae min' fit it wis like yersel'. It's nae easy for a loon 'at his age, Charlie.

CHARLIE Fit wye's it supposed tae be easy? Fin' I wis servin' my time if ye spoke tae a journeyman like 'at bugger 'ere (POINTING IN THE DIRECTION OF ALLAN'S EXIT) ye'd get a clap roon the lug, 'ats fit ye'd get. An ye jist werna late! Fouk were ower feart for thir jobs. A've seen ess table wi' twinty men roon it. Some workin' wi' one han' because they couldna' get richt in aboot. Imagine, streetchin' sidewys tae get in aboot wi' one han' raither than be seen stanin'. You've seen 'at Sam.

SAM Aye, an' the bosses laughin' at it. But I widna' like tae see 'at days again.

KENNY A'm nae sayin' 'at. I'm jist sayin' it's wint too far the ither wye, 'at's a'.

BILL (Looking off UL) Here we go again.

ALLAN ENTERS UL LOOKING AROUND THE TABLE AREA.

ALLAN Far's the fuckin' buns.

BILL Alex's put Kenny on them.

SAM Ivvry chunce o' ye gettin' yer job back though, Allan. I widna worry.

ALLAN I'm nae worried. He can fuckin' hae it. (He joins the table group)

BILL Were ye winchin' last nicht?

ALLAN No, practisin'. Wiv got a big bookin' the night at Methlick. 'Fan did Alex miss mi?

BILL Five minutes ago.

ALLAN Fuck! (HE YAWNS) Fuck this job. (HE BRIGHTENS) Lang lie the morn though. Fuckin' great!

KENNY So yer takin' it are ye?

ALLAN Of course a'm fuckin' takin' it. Did ye think I'm gan tae rise at five o'clock in the mornin' oot o' force o' habit?

CHARLIE Aye, an' maybe now that Kenny's got yer icin' jobby yer plouks'll ging awa.

ALLAN Fit?

CHARLIE Yer ploukes'll ging awa now that yer awa fae the icin'. Ye winna be lickin' at it oany mair. At's fit's giein' ye a' that plouks. Ye ken foo tae get rid 'o them fast, divin't ye?

ALLAN How?

CHARLIE Rub a suppie pish on 'em.

ALLAN Fit?

CHARLIE Aye, get a wee jar or somethin' an' the next time ye ging ti the lavvy pish in it and rub some o't on tae yer face. Yer ploukes'll be awa in a wik. At's right.

ALLAN (LAUGHING) Fuck off!

CHARLIE (SERIOUSLY) Na, a'm tellin' ye. You try a wee suppie pish on yer face an' see.

BILL Sounds like a real country een 'at. Is ess een o' yer Mintlaw tricks Charlie?

CHARLIE Na, nae jist Mintla'.

SAM An' is this something yi've wint in for yersel', Charlie?

CHARLIE Mony a time - fin I hid ploukes.

CHARLIE Er'e ye go now, Allan. Jist ask yer blonnie fit she wints. Ye covered in ploukes or covered in pish.

The men's laughter stops when Alex's voice is heard off.

ALEX Fit the hell's 'at min. In the name o'... Stop, dinna dee oany mair. (HE ENTERS UL WITH A CHELSEA BUN FOLLOWED BY KENNY HOLDING THE POT OF ICING. HE ADDRESSES THE TABLE GROUP) Could neen o' yis hae stopped 'im.

ALLAN Dinna look at me, I wisna here.

ALEX No. If you hid been here you'd be deein' 'em. (TO KENNY) Mix up mair icin'. Preferably wi' a colour that folk can eat withoot spewin' up first.

KENNY GOES OFF DR WITH THE POT AND THE BOTTLE OF FOOD COLOUR.

ALEX cont. (TO ALLAN) You an' me are gan' tae fa' oot lad. Fit's the excuse this mornin'?

ALLAN I'm nae makin' oany.

ALEX An' the yeast tins, did ye forget them again?

ALLAN I must huv.

ALEX Dinna forget them again, okay?

Allan looks down at the pie he is working on and says nothing.

ALEX Right, at eight o'clock ging doon tae the breed plunt for two oors. An' dinna disappear efter, a'll be lookin' for ye. (HE EXITS UR)

ALLAN Bastard! At's me doon 'ere again. I hate 'at place. How's coupin' pan loafs on tae a fuckin'

conveyor belt supposed tae be learnin' yir fuckin' trade (AS HE SPEAKS HE REACHES UNDER THE TABLE AND AFTER A SHORT SEARCH PRODUCES AN EMPTY WATER PISTOL WHICH HE POINTS IN THE DIRECTION OF ALEX'S EXIT). An' washin' tins. Apprentices are jist glorified labourers, 'at's 'a. Same wi' half the jobs in this fuckin' place.

HE EXITS UL.

CHARLIE Far's he awa' till?

BILL Tae fill up his water pistol, I think. Sumb'dy's gan tae get scushed.

CHARLIE It's nae the trade it wis, 'ats for sure. Look at the jobs now far men are jist watchin' machines a' day. They hiv a machine tae dee ess now! (INDICATING THE PIES) Walker's hiv een in.

BILL I noticed the difference in their stuff

CHARLIE Aye, well 'ats fit it is. It's a' gan tae be machines come time. Fit wid we say Sam?

SAM There's still plenty o' jobs for bakers.

CHARLIE Aye but yer sma' bakeries are a' closin doon'. It's jist gan' tae be twa or three big places an' 'at's gan' tae be it! Ers nae gan tae be a trade left in bakin' worth a damn.

DURING THIS ALLAN RETURNS, STUFFING THE FILLED WATER PISTOL INTO HIS BIB.

ALLAN Aye, weel a'm gettin' oot o' this place first chunce I get.

CHARLIE Dinna let yer big break in Methlick ging tae yer heed now, Allan.

ALLAN Na. I'm jinin' the army, a've got a medical next wik. (HE AIMS AND SQUIRTS A JET OF WATER OFFSTAGE)

BILL Fit ye gan tae be - a sniper.

ALLAN Maybe I will. Oanythin' but bakin'. I wis a' afterneen at the recruitin' place yisterdi'.

BILL So ye wint doon right enough. Yer serious then?

ALLAN Too right I'm serious. I'm out o' here pal.

CHARLIE You winna last five minutes in the army, min'.

BILL Fit aboot yer five day wik?

ALLAN (UNCERTAINLY) Ye hiv a five day wik in the army ... once yer trainin's deen.

SAM As lang's 'ers nae a war. Sodjers can fair get killed on a Seterdi if there's a war.

ALLAN Weel, 'ers nae much chunce o' 'ere bein' a war, now is 'ere?

BILL At's fit they telt Charlie in 1939. In't 'at right Charlie?

CHARLIE Aye. Hitler jist completely spiled the regiment's five day wik.

EDDIE ENTERS DL AND GOES TO TAKE A DRINK OF WATER AT THE DRINKING WELL DR. HE NOTICES ALLAN.

EDDIE Oh, yiv shown up hiv ye?

ALLAN Fit's it tae you like?

EDDIE SNORTS AND BENDS DOWN TO DRINK. ALLAN PULLS OUT THE WATER PISTOL AND SQUIRTS IT SO THAT A LITTLE WATER DROPS ON EDDIE'S HEAD. HE HIDES THE PISTOL IMMEDIATELY. EDDIE LOOKS UP AT THE ROOF.

EDDIE (TO THE TABLE GROUP) They should get 'at roof sorted y'now. It's the same doon at the ovens. The place is fa'in apairt.

Allan looks down at his work as do the rest. Bill fails to keep a straight face.

EDDIE cont.   (AS HE CROSSES L) I dinna see the fun in't, Bill. It

winna be the first time sumb'dy's slipped on the fleer for water comin' in the roof.

BILL (RECOVERING) No, right enough, Eddie. Aye the sooner we move doon tae the new place the better.

EDDIE Can I hae that pies doon tae the ovens? I've a pile o' stuff nae handy tae fire the day.

ALLAN Tak' 'em wi' ye, seen's yer gan' at wye.

EDDIE Listen you, ye cheeky ...

BILL (QUICKLY) Aye, nae bother Eddie. (TO ALLAN) Tak' them doon. (ALLAN STARTS TO PROTEST) Jist shut it. Tak' them doon. (TO EDDIE, WINKING AND POINTING TO THE TOP PAN OF PIES ON THE RACK) THE SPECIALS.

ALLAN EXITS UL WITH THE RACK OF PIES. EDDIE EXITS DL.

BILL (LAUGHING) Jesus Christ, leakin' roof! At loon's aff he's heed. Now I ken ess is a dyin' trade.

SAM Aye, but a'ts fire he's playin' wi' there Charlie, nae watter. (HE EXITS DL)

CHARLIE He's gan' tae get his heed tae play wi' 'at loon. Eddie's nae sum'bdy tae play wi' these days.

BILL Och. He's aye been a sour bugger.

CHARLIE Na, na, I've seen a change in 'im.

ALLAN RETURNS UR.

ALLAN Fa's 'at pan o' pies for wi' the special mince? (HE CROSSES TO THE DRINKER DR)

BILL It's a special order.

ALLAN I widnae mind een for mi breakfast.

BILL You leave them alone, sonny boy.

DURING THIS ALLAN DRINKS AND USEEN BY THE TABLE GROUP HE UNSCREWS THE DRINKER'S SPOUT BEFORE RETURNING TO THE TABLE.

ALLAN You a' hae een.

BILL At's got nithin' tae dee wi' you. You mind yer ain business aboot fit folk hae for their breakfast an' dinna you touch 'at pies, a' right?

CHARLIE I'd of thought ye'd huv fancied the band side o' the army fit wi' you bein' a musician?

KENNY ENTER UR AND THE GROUP

ALLAN Na, min, 'at's nae my kin' o' music.

CHARLIE So fit aboot yer group? Yi'd be gie'n' a' that up.

ALLAN A'll jine een in the army. The boy at the recruitin' office says 'ers lots o' pop groups in the army. I might start a new band. I'll see fit kin' o' music their playin'.

KENNY Music? Ye ca' thon shite music. I watched yer Top o' the Pops last nicht, oan's jist a racket.

CHARLIE Fa' wis 'at darkie quine. (HE STARTS TO SING IN COMIC FASHION) "My girl lollipop, my boy lollipop." Helen Shapiro wis it or somethin'?

BILL At wis Millie ye feel bugger.

CHARLIE Aye, weel I kent it wisna Vera Lynne.

KENNY Now 'ers a real singer for ye.

ALLAN Jesus! Vera Lynne. Get a grip. It's the sixties min ... (HE IS DISTRACTED BY THE ENTRANCE OF SAM DL)

SAM (LOOKING AROUND) Far's the trolly? There it is. (HE MOVES DOWN TO COLLECT IT AND CROSSES TO EXIT DR. ALLAN IS FOCUSED ON THE DRINKER)

BILL Fit aboot 'Bothy Nichts' then Kenny? Dae ye watch 'at? You will Charlie, a country loon like you.

ALLAN (With exaggerated "country" accent) Michty aye, the Kennethmont Loons an' Quines.

BILL (Also with accent) Come awa in Greive.

ALLAN (Continuing with the accent) Aye, come awa wi' ye. Tak' aff yer jaeket an' gies a bla on yir jews harp ... but wash yer han's an' dee up yer flies first ye foul auld bastard.

They all laugh except for Kenny. Eddie enters UL and crosses and exit UR. Kenny sees him and looks up at the clock.

KENNY (Disgusted) A'm awa for mi tea.

ALLAN (Holding up an empty pie case) Dinna forget yer brose bowl. (With the accent again) The Grumpian TV Brose Bowl.

BILL Kenny's nae exactly a bunnel o' laughs is he?

CHARLIE Nae the same since his wife left 'im.

BILL Wi' the lodger.

ALLAN (Laughing) Is 'at right?

CHARLIE Aye. He wis night shift in the breed at the time an' took nae weel. He's pit hame aboot two in the mornin' and guess in fa's bed he finds the lodger? Fit a gipe, eh? Imagine leavin' for yir work at half past ten at night an' wavin cheerio tae the wife an' the lodger. "Well, goodnight yous two, see yis in the mornin'."

BILL He breeds poodles dis he nae?

ALLAN Fit!? Poodles?

CHARLIE I think it's poodles he breeds. Sam has a dog fae him. He judges at dog shows y'ken. Oh, he kens hes stuff. Travels a' owre judgin' at the shows.

Sam enters DR with the trolly loaded.

CHARLIE Sam, fit kin' o' dogs dis Kenny breed?

SAM (Stopping) Poodles. (Jokingly) Why, were ye thinkin' about gettin' een? (He turns to the drinker and bends down to drink)

CHARLIE No, no thanks...

Sam jumps back as a strong jet of water hits him full in the face. He turns to Allan who is unable to conceal his delight.

SAM (Angrily wiping his face with his sleeves) That was you again.

ALLAN Fit? How dae ye ken' it wis me? I nivver touched the thing. Fit wye am I aye blamed?

SAM (Sam shakes his head and screws the spout back on. He collects the trolly and exits DL) Bloody apprentices

Allan goes to the drinker, unscrews the spout again and returns to the table.

CHARLIE Hemin', pit that spoot back on afore somb'dy rips yer heed aff.

BILL (Looking off and laughing) Here's Alex wi' the wages, better pit it back on pal.

ALLAN Fuckin' leave it.

Alex enters with a shallow box containing pay packets. He also has a pad and pencil. As he gives each person their wage packet he takes down names. This is for those working overtime on Saturday morning.

ALEX Seterdi', Bill?

BILL Aye.

ALEX Charlie?

CHARLIE Aye.

Sam enters DL and joins the table group.

ALEX Sam?

SAM I canna, Alex.

ALEX Allan?

ALLAN (Who has been looking on puzzled) Fit's 'ess for?

ALEX Seterdi mornin'. For yer overtime on Seterdi mornin'?

ALLAN Yer jokin'! I'm nae working on Seterdi.

ALEX Aye, yer gettin' double time for it, three hoors at double time.

ALLAN A'm nae wintin double time, I'm wintin' Seterdi aff. At's fit wiv been workin' extra hoors durin' the wik for. Fit's goin' on. I'm nae workin' on Seterdi.

ALEX Ye'll come in the morn if I need ye tae come in the morn.

ALLAN Like fuck I will.

ALEX Look, a'm nae arguin' wi' ye. (He starts to write Allan's name in the book)

ALLAN Dinna pit my name doo in 'ere.

ALEX (Putting away the book) Right, tell it tae Thompson. (He exits DR)

ALLAN Fit's 'ess shite aboot. Naeb'dy telt me oanythin' aboot ess.

SAM Well ye should have been. Some work still has to be done on Saturday. Ye canna' refuse to work overtime. The place couldna' operate if we didna' work overtime. Imagine fit wid happen at Cristmas if ab'dy wint hame. The place'd be oot ' business.

ALLAN But, 'ess is crazy. Fit your sayin' is that tae get a five day wik yiv tae work overtime on a Seterdi.

At's the day yir wintin' aff. Yer
still workin' six days. Ess is a lot
o' shite. I'm nae comin' in. I'm
gan tae see Thompson now. (HE
MAKES TO LEAVE)

SAM No dinna dee that.   He's
jist gan' tae back his foreman.
Look, leave it jist now.   Ye hivna
jist exactly went aboot tacklin' Alex
very dipomatically have ye? Jist keep
away fae him jist now. Leave it
wi' me. (HE EXITS).

ALLAN You boys nivver said
oanythin' tae me aboot 'ess.
Fucksake, yiv a' been ravin aboot
the five day wik like it wis som'n'
great.   A' yiv really been wintin'
is double time on a Seterdi.

BILL Look, jist calm yersel' doon.
Alex's got plenty o' men for fit
needs tae be deen the morn.
You've got his back up 'at's a'.
Naebody's gan' tae mak' ye come
in the morn's mornin'.

ALLAN You're fuckin' right thir
pal. I dinna get you boys ava.

BILL At's because ye hivna a clue
fit it's like tae bring up a family
on twelve punds a wik! I canna
afford tae lie in my bed on a Seterdi
mornin' if I can make some extra.
(HE LOOKS OFF UR) Watch oot. Here's
Thompson comin' (TO ALLAN) You
keep awa fae 'im.

THE TABLE FALLS SILENT AS ALEX AND THOMPSON
ENTER DR AND CROSS TO THE DESK TO LOOK
AT THE ORDER SHEETS.   THE SOUND OF THE
MIXING MACHINES IN THE BACKGROUND
INCREASES SO THAT THEIR CONVERSATION IS
NOT HEARD.   THOMPSON TURNS AND WALKS
TOWARDS THE DRINKER.   ALEX CONTIUES TO
LOOK AT THE ORDER SHEETS.   THE TABLE GROUP
LOOK ON AS THOMPSON BENDS TO TAKE A DRINK.
THEY FREEZE AS HE STRAIGHTENS AND JUMPS
BACK IN ALARM AS A JET OF WATER HITS HIM
FULL IN THE FACE.

THE MIXING MACHINE NOISE IS RAISED FURTHER
AND THE LIGHTS FADE OUT.

END OF SCENE AND ACT ONE.

Buchan's Kirks
Christine Ritchie

Grey granite, square agin the icy blast
At blaws sna' n hale watter ower i lan,
Nivir settlin' ti hap pairk nor howe
Atween grey hulls an saut grey wrunklt sea.

Fisher kirkies heich abeen spray wash't grey
toons
Scourin' seas aneth for wannert sauls
Firm agin the micht o' livin' gales
At ettle sair ti rock their steadfast foons.

Ferm kirks, amang grey nets o' drysteen waas
Cast ower green girse, fite tattie flooers an'
gowden corn,
Haulin' the faith fu' in aboot ti hear
the black-cleed wyvers o the Godspell threids.

Rummles o steens far eence stood bastion waas
Fornent the walkin' o' the Druid steens
Grey monks pintin' texts in reed an gowd
Ti haud awa the lowe o' Beltane fires.

A Good Age
Marjory Nicholson

Parent rears child.
And
Child rears parent
To a right good age.
Sudden
Confusion when death
Leaves parent,
The panic-stricken
Waif howling
In helpless despair.

Accidental Sonnet

Marjory Nicholson

Hiv ye ivver made a jigsa an i hinmist bit wis tint?
Hiv ye ivver taen a hem up jist tae fin ye'd daen it squint?
Hiv ye queued up at i checkoot an fun oot ye hid nae money?
Hiv ye ivver watch't a comedy at wisna even funny?
Hiv ye gaen ontil a diet - an ye fun a stane nae lost it?
Ah bet yer coupon aye comes up the wik ye dinna post it?
An fin ye're wyvin ganzies, div ye aye rin oot o wool?
Did ye tak richt smashin photies fin i camera nott a spool?
An ah bet it's aye yer washin at gets soakit wi i rain?
An ye ayewis see a bargain fin ye've naething left tae spen!
Lookin back, ye're awfa lucky cos yer trauchles hiv been few.
Some fowk wid gie their ee-teeth jist tae hae a life like you.
Aye, we really maun be thankfu that wir lives hiv been sae rare.
We've hid some disappeintments, bit wis ony o em sair?

Ah Wish Ah Hid A Fiver

Marjory Nicholson

Ah wish ah hid a fiver
For ilky time ah've said
The day ah'll dae the ironin
An hoover a'neath the bed.
Ah'm ful o good intentions -
Ye hiv tae gie me that
Bit fit's a suppie caddis?
Ah wis playin wi the cat!!

Ah'm gaun tae wash the windies
Ah'll hae tae clean the brass
Is at somebody at the door?
Come in, sit doon, ma lass.
Of course ah'm nae ower busy
Tae listen tae yer crack
Ah'll jist pit on the kettle
Tak aff yer coat, sit back.

Is at i time? Fa's carin?
Dinna rush awa - Ye're worrit
Fit's a'dae, aul freen -
Ah've kent ye far ower lang.
Ere's something ye're nae sayin
So dinna tell me lees.
Ye ken ah'm here tae listen
So tell me at yer ease.

Nivver mine yer ironin
Or hooverin a'neath yer bed
Ye're hidin something fae me
So spit at oot instead.
Ye've fun a lumpie in yer briest
Noo dinna worry quine
It winna be malignant
Ah bet it's jist benign.

It seems like only yesterday
We took the cancer on
Fanivver it got near the goal
The bugger scored an won.
It fairly wis malignant
The lumpie that ye fun
Cancer on the rampage,
Cancer on the run.

Aul freen, ye're jist a memory
A milestane in the past.
Ye held ma haun - cos I wis feart -
Until ye breathed yer last.
Next time ah mak ma wishes
Ah winna ask for wealth
Fit the hell's a fiver
If ye hinna got yer health?

BREAKING NEW
GROUND
shortlisted,
short story

Under The Sun
Christine M Ritchie

The bridge was the frontier. Before the bridge, his mind had been filled with thoughts of schoolwork still to be done, staff to deal with. Some had queried, and even spoken out against, his policies. What did they know, locked in the safety of their own departments? He had the responsibility of running the school. Talking is easy, but he had important decisions to make.

But, as his eyes and spirits followed the ranked peaks of the Highlands, blue in the early evening, the bridge seemed to him like a symbol. On the other side his stresses would disappear and he would enter a carefree land where he would be renewed and refreshed.

It was a long drive for a Friday evening but Alan had decided that he would reach his destination that night. He had a long weekend and was going to make the most of it. This way, he would have two whole days in the hills before he need contemplate the return journey.

The bridge arced high above the Firth. To his right he could see the flat coastal lands running on into forgotten distance; just below, to his left, the town sat astride its river and sprawled beyond, amoeba-like, settling itself into every available piece of flat land and now reaching out over the hillsides beyond. The Firth stretched far and dark, toward the hills, the land of his fathers. He rather liked the sound of that, cliché though it was - the land of his fathers.

As he continued on his journey, his horizons shrank until he existed only in the tunnel of the night driver. At last, in hazy, swimming weariness, he arrived, performed what was necessary and slept cocooned in fresh polyester, his jaded senses faintly recognising the scents of thyme and honeysuckle wafting gently through his half-opened window.

Refreshed and ready for action, he rose, breakfasted heartily and strode out on a dewy morning which promised to mature into a day of generous warmth. Alan took the road which led up the glen towards the high moors. He thought of little, simply revelled in being part of this ancient land of hill and burn and heather, where his folk had lived in days gone by. He fancied that the land was drawing him on, into its midst, taking a son to its bosom. It was a new experience, titillating in its way, strangely exciting. Yet, he had never given the place a thought before, although of course he had always known that this was the hereditary territory of his clan chief. He had never in his life attended Clan Gatherings, always considering them a little chi-chi, a vehicle for the unbridled nostalgia of third generation Americans.

The glen had now closed about him. Veering off the path, he climbed up the hillside until he came to a pile of stones scattered randomly around. Sitting on one of the bigger ones he gazed about him with a sigh of deep contentment - lord of all he surveyed. If he had been the clan chief all this land would have belonged to him. He tried to will himself into the persona of the chief looking out over his land. Surprisingly he found it not too difficult.

The feeling, he decided, was very similar to that which he experienced in regarding his own school. Musing complacently on this happy coincidence, his attention gradually found a focus, through a consistent, niggling rear attack, on the stones on which he sat. His gaze now began to home in on other such heaps of stones scattered around the braes, overgrown with grass and heather so that some were evident only as green mounds - fairy knolls, he might have thought in more whimsical mood.

Realisation crept up as if the knowledge had been with him always. These stones were all that remained of the homes of the crofters who had been evicted during the infamous Highland Clearances. He found an unsuspected anger welling up from a source deep and forgotten inside himself. His ancestors had been put out of their homes - for sheep! All that they had built up over centuries, livings wrested from the hard land that they knew and loved, destroyed in one fell swoop. It was worse than the Holocaust. The Jews had died; his people had had to suffer a living death on a hostile coast. The chief had betrayed them, and the factor, self-seeking and power-hungry, was no better - obeying orders, the old, old excuse.

Filled with a righteous anger that slopped warmly and pleasantly around his heart, Alan tramped on up the glen. And in this rich mulch, an embryonic idea grew and blossomed. In his school, pupils should and would be taught about their own land and people in their History lessons. All his first and second year pupils would be taught about Culloden and the Clearances and their far-reaching effects on the people. The English Department would read literature dealing with this period and the Music Department would teach Jacobite songs and songs of the exiles to Canada and America. He became more and more excited as the idea grew. He would be a pioneer in Education - a man for the people. He would address conclaves of headmasters and point out the comparative irrelevance of the Battle of Jutland to children who did not know their own history and culture and thus could not come to terms with themselves. He would be hailed as the innovator - the One who made all the old basic values new and alive and relevant to present day society, an on-going initiative in integrated learning. All this liaison between departments would be so good for everybody - get his staff off their complacent backsides - always complaining that he did not take the trouble to become acquainted with their courses!

Alan fairly floated over tussocky heather, bogs and boulders in his sturdy walking boots, occasionally trampling nevertheless on the delicate moorland cannoch and bruising the bog myrtle to release its evocative, bitter-sweet fragrance.

He slept soundly that night, exhausted and satisfied - no longer subject to the escapism of the previous night but with the inner contentment of one who has come to terms with his roots and who would use this self-knowledge to move forward with a new impetus in his career.

The next day it rained - not your Scotch mist but a flood, a deluge, a total Spring-clean of the clouds.

Alan did not experience the anticipated sinking of the spirits. As he ate his excellent breakfast in the comfortable, family-owned hotel, he asked his landlord about the evictions from the glens. His host replied that he did not himself have a very detailed knowledge of the subject but that he kept a good stock of books on local history and wildlife etc. in the residents' lounge. With a wry glance at the wall of water outside the window, he observed that he found it necessary to provide some stimulating reading for his guests.

Alan therefore found himself comfortably ensconced in a deep leather armchair in front of a roaring fire, with a pile of books on a small mahogany table at his elbow, partnered variously as the day wore on by coffee and cakes, tea and sandwiches and several large malt whiskies.

He had a wonderful day, relaxed and content, researching and soaking up facts and Glenfarclas alternately and growing comfortably angry, as any Highlander should, as he read through the lists of those who had been evicted from the homeland:

Murdo McKay, crofter
Angus McKay, crofter
William Chisholm, tinker
Donald McBeth, crofter
George McDonald, crofter
William Sutherland, schoolteacher

He felt drawn to William Sutherland and suffered with him as he sat all night on the green hillside and watched his dwelling, "smouldering into ashes." He read too of the brave Ross women - Margaret Ross, Ann Ross, Catherine Ross - who had fought for their homes and been murdered brutally for their temerity.

More and more he had the feeling within him of a Great Mission. Nothing had ever moved him so much. He felt so positive, so full of energy. That night he drifted off to sleep on a cloud of euphoria, on an arrow swiftly flying to the centre of things.

As he set off southwards next morning, he felt no laggardly dragging of the feet, no sense of regret at leaving this wonderful place, his inspiration.

He had thought that he would hate the prospect of returning to school but instead he had experienced a catharsis. He could hardly wait for the beginning to begin...

Routine jobs could not depress him this Tuesday morning. He would leap through them like a Landseer stag. First he asked his secretary to send memos to the Principal Teachers of History, English and Music, requesting them to attend a meeting in his office at ten thirty to discuss courses.

Now, to routine business. He had been told that he was over-staffed. The school must shed five teachers, to be transferred to other schools in the region. As Headmaster, he must choose the departments which would lose staff and name the individual teachers, last in to their departments, to be designated for compulsory transfer. He did not suppose that they would be too happy, especially those who had been at the school for some time. Still, they knew the rules. This was national policy.

Kenneth McMillan, teacher of Geography
Mary Sim, teacher of English
Donald Munro, teacher of History
Catherine Ross, teacher of Home Economics
John McKay, teacher of Music

Impatiently he wrote the names, wanting to be finished, to get on with the real, important business. He could not help smiling in anticipation.

"Ah, have my principal teachers arrived, Miss Sellar? Show them in..."

Macduff times 3.

Ian Crockatt

1.

From east of Macduff I saw west of Banff
a field's pelt blown to the clouds,
the brown of it brawling down cliffs and out

to sea. 4 miles off the fishers
netted a dustbowl, and the shy sun
hid her head in a fine-tilthed veil.

2.

Make slits of your eyes.
Look at the scrambled-egg fields
above Macduff. Can such yellows be real?

As rape is. As unrequited love.
As drinking alone is.
As stone walls, Macduff.

3.

In 'the hovel', Macduff,
3 men grinned and fluttered their paper poems.
Gulls on the slates exchanged ecstatic squeals.

Macduff is where I learnt
how boats are built the lost way,
and how exiles feel.

Civilised Man

James Duthie

Review and Biographical Information
by Greg Dawson Allen

Mobil

joint winner of
1994 MOBIL
SCOTTISH
PLAYWRIGHTS'
COMPETITION

"The events of a pre-peace initiative Ireland spill over to the coast of Buchan as the sitting room of a cottar house becomes the setting for a hostage situation involving a Government minister snatched amid bloody scenes from a fishing holiday on the banks of the Ugie, and Effie, a resilient, recently bereaved widow.

Their captors, part of an IRA cell in mainland Scotland, become frustrated at unsuccessful attempts to move them from their randomly chosen hiding place.

'Civilised Man' begs the question why conflict in war affects not only those fighting for King (or Queen) and country but those who, sometimes decades or years later, become part of their lives. Yet the play offers no answers or solutions, nor attempts to do so. There are none. Only the reality of commitment to a cause and the focus on striving to win at any cost.

It is also a study of four characters from different backgrounds thrown together in an isolated cottage who, in some way or another, have suffered loss.

This is not a play, outdated by present political moves, but a metaphor for the underlying personal agendas which each of the politicians carries to the negotiating table. "....the past yields the answer to the present."

James Duthie was born a War baby in Haddo House near Tarves, which was then in use as a hospital. Signing on a drift netter as tenth man at the age of fifteen, he has spent almost his entire life at the fishing, earning a living which latterly came to subsidise his writing.

An ambition to write for television was realised in the mid 1970s when his first screenplay 'Donnal and Sally', a love story set in the Willowbank special needs centre near Peterhead, was broadcast on BBC Scotland. Besides bringing actors Gerrard Kelly and Gregor Fisher to public attention, 'Donnal and Sally' won the 'Director's Award' at the Prague Festival. Another television screenplay followed, again set in the north east - 'The Drystane Dyker', which went on to collect the 'Harry Govan Memorial Award'.

The onset of Crone's disease prevented Jim completing a specially commissioned thirteen part series, 'The Buchans of Buchan', focusing on the lives of a fictional family.

Although by his own admission preferring the freedom of writing for the camera, 'Civilised Man' is his first script for the stage. Not surprisingly, Jim has collected yet another award, this time becoming a shared winner of the Mobil Scottish Playwrights' Award 1994."

CAST:

EFFIE
widow, early sixties.
DANNY
member of the IRA, nineteen.
COMMANDER
member of the IRA, late forties.
GM
government minister, forties.

SET:

The living room of a cottar house in Buchan. The room has a window centre stage, a door leading to hallway and kitchen, and a door leading to bedroom. Furniture, sofa, armchair, table, two chairs, a wall photograph of a young soldier, television and a suit of clothes on a coat-hanger.

❖

SCENE 1

NIGHT. OFF-STAGE THE FAINT SOUND OF A MOTOR CAR APPROACHING THE HOUSE.

EFFIE, RECENTLY WIDOWED, IS STANDING AT THE TABLE GOING THROUGH A FEW MEMENTOS OF HER LIFE WITH HER LATE HUSBAND (SANDY) - LETTERS, PHOTOGRAPHS, ETC. EVENTUALLY COMING ACROSS TWO MILITARY MEDALS, SHOWING THERE IS A CONNECTION BY LOOKING AT THE PHOTOGRAPH OF SANDY AS A YOUNG MAN IN ARMY UNIFORM HANGING ON THE WALL, JUST SHOWING A LITTLE EMOTION, THEN PUTS MEDALS ETC. INTO A CARDBOARD BOX, PICKS IT UP AND SLOWLY EXITS TO BEDROOM.

OFF   SOUND OF MOTOR CAR GETTING LOUDER

EFFIE   (PAUSING TO REGISTER SOUND AS SHE EXITS)

OFF   CAR ENGINE MISFIRING SEVERAL TIMES AS ITS SPLUTTERS TO A HALT OUTSIDE THE HOUSE, CAR IGNITION BEING TRIED UNSUCCESSFULLY SEVERAL TIMES. CAR DOORS BEING SLAMMED SHUT ACCOMPANIED BY THE URGENT AND ANXIOUS VOICE OF DANNY AND THE CALM VOICE OF THE COMMANDER. TWO IRA MEN WHO HAVE ABDUCTED A GOVERNMENT MINISTER. THE ABDUCTION HAS GONE WRONG, RESULTING IN TWO IRA MEN AND TWO SECURITY GUARDS

BEING KILLED. AND NOW THE CAR HAS BROKEN DOWN BEYOND REPAIR.

EFFIE   (ENTERS DRAWN BY THE SOUND, HURRIES TO THE WINDOW TO INVESTIGATE)

OFF   SOUND OF DANNY AND THE COMMANDER ENTERING THE HOUSE. EFFIE ON HER WAY TO THE HALLWAY DOOR WHEN IT BURSTS OPEN AND THE COMMANDER, GUN IN HAND, STORMS INTO THE ROOM, GRABBING HER AROUND THE NECK AND PRESSING GUN INTO HER HEAD.

DANNY   (UNARMED, STANDS PANIC-STRICKEN IN DOORWAY)

COMMANDER   (INDICATING HE SHOULD SEARCH THE OTHER ROOMS)

DANNY   (INSTINCTIVELY ACKNOWLEDGING, HE EXITS KITCHEN)

EFFIE   (STRUGGLING)

COMMANDER   (PUSHING GUN HARDER INTO HER HEAD)

DANNY   (BRIEF PAUSE ENTERING)
Kitchen, e-hh..no one there.

COMMANDER   (GESTURING WITH GUN

TO BEDROOM)

DANNY   (HURRYING TO BEDROOM)

COMMANDER   (HISSING) Yer gun.

DANNY   (HAULING GUN FROM WAISTBAND AS HE EXITS)

COMMANDER   (COCKING GUN) I said, I wanted t'know, how many there are in the house. (PUSHING GUN INTO HER FACE)

EFFIE   (SHOUTING DESPERATELY) Naebody else, jist me, honest t'God - honest t'God!

DANNY   (OFF SHOUTING) She's lyin'!

EFFIE   (DENYING VEHEMENTLY) Honest t'God I'm nae, (SHOUTING) I'm nae!

DANNY   (ENTERING, CARRYING A SUIT ON A HANGER, HOLDS UP TO HER DEMANDING AN EXPLANATION)

EFFIE (ON SEEING HER HUSBAND'S SUIT, OVERCOME WITH EMOTION)

COMMANDER Whose is it?

EFFIE (CRYING) My husband's.

DANNY (THROWING SUIT ON TABLE AS HE GOES AND GRABS HER)

COMMANDER Where is he?

DANNY (GRABBING HER) Is there a car in the garage outside, a truck, transport o' any kind?

EFFIE (OVERWHELMED, UNABLE TO REPLY)

DANNY (SHOUTING) Do ye have a car?

EFFIE (CRYING)

DANNY (SHAKING HER) Do ye have a car for chrissake?

EFFIE My husband's deid, he died last week.

DANNY Do ye have a bluddy car?

COMMANDER Go and check out the garage.

EFFIE There's nae car.

DANNY Chrrist!

COMMANDER Check it out.

DANNY Didn't ye hear what she said?

COMMANDER Do what the fughin hell yer told.

DANNY (EXITS DISGRUNTLED)

COMMANDER (ESCORTS EFFIE TO THE ARMCHAIR)

EFFIE My husband is dead, and there's nae car.

COMMANDER (IGNORES HER; INDICATES SHE SIT)

EFFIE If it's money.

COMMANDER (SILENCES HER, SHORT PAUSE, WHISPERING) I'm going to ask you a few questions. (RIGHT INTO HER FACE) And you're to give me the right answers. Understand?

EFFIE (FRIGHTENEDLY ACKNOWLEDGES)

COMMANDER (SHORT PAUSE) I want to know.

DANNY (ENTERING IN A STATE) There's no car, what are we goin' to do, how are we to get away from here?

COMMANDER (CALMLY) We don't.

DANNY We can't stay here, what if anyone calls, e-hh the police and the military will be searching the whole country and ...

COMMANDER We stay here until we get further orders.

DANNY Orders? Brigade headquarters don't know we're here.

COMMANDER Stop yer crawthumpin' and bring the prisoner in.

EFFIE Prisoner?

DANNY Give's a hand then.

COMMANDER Go and get him in.

DANNY He's a great big heavy bugger.

COMMANDER For fughsake!

DANNY (PROTESTING EXITS)

EFFIE Who are you people?

COMMANDER Who we are doesn't concern you. Understand?

EFFIE (FRIGHTENEDLY ACKNOWLEDGES)

COMMANDER (PAUSE, POINTS GUN AT HER) Yer husband's dead ye say?

EFFIE (CONFIRMS)

COMMANDER What about your family?

EFFIE (INDICATING PHOTO ON WALL) Sandy an' me, we'd nae faimily ... nae bairns o' oor ain.

COMMANDER (BRIEF PAUSE) What of relatives, do they visit often?

EFFIE Very seldom, there's none live near.

COMMANDER With your bereavement, some would've called to pay their respects?

EFFIE Some did.

COMMANDER And I expect some will be callin' again?

EFFIE (WITH GROWING INDIGNATION) If you want to know the truth there were precious few o' oor so-called relatives came an' paid their respects. The few that did, I didna expect, and them that I'd looked for ... (REALISING THE FUTILITY OF IT) Fit's a' this questions for?

COMMANDER Just answer. What of friends, neighbours?

EFFIE Oor nearest neighbours are in the toon, ower a mile awa.

COMMANDER Do any o' them call on a regular basis?

EFFIE (DENYING)

COMMANDER No one at all?

EFFIE Folks here tend to keep themselves to themselves, if there's trouble or illness it's different. When Sandy was lyin' ill ...

COMMANDER Yes-yes. (GOING TO HALLWAY DOOR, CALLS) What's keepin' ye?

DANNY (OFF, GASPING) If ye'd give's a bluddy hand here.

COMMANDER (TO HER) What about postmen, milkman, any others who may call?

EFFIE The milkman's the only one who calls regularly.

COMMANDER What time?

EFFIE Six in the mornin'.

COMMANDER Every morning?

EFFIE Aye, except Sunday.

COMMANDER You're sure it's six?

EFFIE Aye, I'm sure, Sandy used to ... (VOICE FALLING AWAY ON MENTIONING HUSBAND) call him oor alarm clock.

DANNY (BRIEF PAUSE, OFF, SHOUTS) A-h geeza a hand here wi' this fugher will ye?

COMMANDER Sit there! (BEGINS EXIT, PAUSING) And don't dare move. Not an inch. Understand? (EXITS)

EFFIE (AFRAID BUT GIVING IN TO HER CURIOSITY, GETS UP AND GOES TO THE DOOR. JUST AS SHE REACHES IT SHE HEARS THEM RE-ENTER HOUSE AND HURRIES BACK TO HER CHAIR) PAUSE, THE COMMANDER AND DANNY ENTER CARRYING THE DRUGGED GOVERNMENT MINISTER WHO IS DRESSED IN RIVER CLOTHES, WEARING THIGH-WADERS ETC. DANNY CONFIDENCE RETURNING IS WEARING GM'S FISHING HAT STUCK ON HIS HEAD AT A JAUNTY ANGLE. EFFIE WATCHING THEM WITH AN AIR OF DISBELIEF AS THEY DUMP HIM ON THE FLOOR NEAR HER.

COMMANDER (GASPING WITH RELIEF)

DANNY Didn't I tell ye he as a weighty bugger? (TAKING OFF HAT AND DROPPING IT ON GM) Just a Brit full o' the proverbial.

GM (MOANS)

EFFIE (CONCERNED)

DANNY A'h he's alright Ma, just had somethin' to make him sleep.

EFFIE Who is he?

COMMANDER (TAKING HANDCUFFS FROM POCKET) Quiet ye ould biddy. (PUTTING CUFFS ON) Get the car into the garage.

DANNY I'll never manage on me own.

COMMANDER The car.

DANNY (GETS THE MESSAGE, EXITS HURRIEDLY)

COMMANDER D'ye have a telephone?

EFFIE (REFRAINS FROM ANSWERING)

COMMANDER (SLOWLY GETTING UP, MENACINGLY) Do you have a telephone?

EFFIE (DEFIANTLY REFUSING TO ANSWER)

COMMANDER (GRABBING HER BY THE HAIR)

EFFIE (TERRIFIED) No!

COMMANDER (BRIEF PAUSE, LETS HER GO)

EFFIE (DESPAIRING) Why did you hiv to come here?

COMMANDER (KEEPING UP INTIMIDATION) Just answer my questions. Understand?

GM (SLOWLY REGAINING CONSCIOUSNESS, ATTEMPTING TO GET UP)

EFFIE (INSTINCTIVELY GOING TO ASSIST HIM)

COMMANDER (SHOVING HER BACK INTO HER CHAIR) You don't go near him. Understand?

EFFIE No I didna understand, yi-yi coorse broot (EMOTIONAL). If my Sandy were still alive he'd ... he'd gee yi short-shrift.

DANNY (LEANING IN THE DOORWAY, GASPING) Ye'll have to give's a hand wi' that fughin car.

COMMANDER (GESTURING TO GM) He's comin' out o' it, can't ye manage?

DANNY M'ballocks are at me feet man.

COMMANDER (HURRIEDLY CHECKS GM'S LEVEL OF CONSCIOUSNESS BY SLAPPING HIM ON THE FACE, TO DANNY) Is the back door locked?

DANNY Dunno.

COMMANDER Check it. (GETTING UP) Don't want her runnin' out on us. (TAKING A FIRM HOLD OF EFFIE) Don't go near him ... don't go near him. Understand?

EFFIE (ACKNOWLEDGING)

COMMANDER (SHOUTS) Have ye locked the door?

DANNY (APPEARING IN THE DOORWAY) Locked and bolted Commander sur.

COMMANDER (USHERING DANNY OUT AS HE EXITS)

EFFIE Commander, huh!

GM (MOANING AS HE REGAINS CONSCIOUSNESS, GROGGY. PULLING AT HANDCUFFS AS HE ATTEMPTS TO GET UP)

EFFIE (CASTS A FRIGHTENED EYE AT THE DOOR, HESITATES, THEN GOES TO ASSIST HIM) Canny, jist canny noo ... easy (PLACING CUSHION BELOW HIS HEAD).

GM U-hh-o-hh ... who?

EFFIE Shhh! (MAKING HIM COMFORTABLE)

GM (BRIEF PAUSE) U-hh ... who are you?

EFFIE (LOOKING ANXIOUSLY AT DOOR, WHISPERING) The men that took you here are outside, their car has broken doon, they forced their way in here.

GM (ACKNOWLEDGING) Where am I?

EFFIE In a cottar hoose a gweed mile fae Peterheid.

GM Peterhead.

DANNY, COMMANDER (OFF, ENTERING HOUSE)

EFFIE (BACKING OFF TO HER CHAIR) They said not to go near you.

DANNY (ENTERING) A-h his nibs is awake. (MOCKINGLY SALUTING) Did ye sleep well mister Government Minister?

GM Hmmph!

DANNY (HALTING BESIDE HIM) Had ye a good fishin'-trip? Caught more than you bargained for, eh?

GM What's happened to my two security men?

DANNY Ye mean the two SAS scumbags? O-h they're takin' swimmin' lessons from the fish in the river Ugie.

COMMANDER (ENTERING)

GM You've murdered them?

DANNY (GRABBING GM) Two o' our men were murdered ye bastard.

EFFIE (ON HER FEET) Leave him aleen.

COMMANDER (INTERVENING)

DANNY I'll kill the bastard.

COMMANDER (PUSHING HIM TOWARDS WINDOW) Go and keep a watch at the window.

DANNY (RELUCTANTLY GOING) Bastard!

GM (TO COMMANDER) Look I e-h know that you'll do what you want with me, but I demand that you release the old lady she's no ...

COMMANDER You demand fugh-all!

GM (ABOUT TO PROTEST)

COMMANDER (GESTURING TO DANNY) Or would you rather I turned him loose on ye? (PICKING UP CUSHION, HOLDING OUT TO EFFIE WITHOUT LOOKING AT HER) The next time you disobey my orders, will be yer last. (TURNING AND THRUSTING CUSHION AT HER) Understand?

EFFIE (ACKNOWLEDGING SLUMPS DOWN IN CHAIR)

DANNY (GESTURING AT TELEVISION SET) Isn't it about time for the news yet?

COMMANDER (CHECKS TIME, THEN SWITCHES ON TV, NOTHING HAPPENING, GIVES TV A THUMP, CHECKS WALL SWITCH, GIVES IT ANOTHER THUMP)

EFFIE (SMUGLY) It disna work.

COMMANDER (THUMPING TV IN FRUSTRATION) Have ye a radio?

EFFIE In the bedroom.

COMMANDER (GOES TO BEDROOM)

EFFIE (WAITING UNTIL HE IS IN BEDROOM DOORWAY) It disna work either.

COMMANDER (FURIOUS GOES AND GRABS HER BY THE HAIR) Don't try and get clever wi' me wumman.

EFFIE (CRYING OUT IN PAIN)

GM (ATTEMPTING TO GET UP) Let her be.

DANNY (ALREADY ON HIS WAY UP, DRAWING GUN, PUSHING GM BACK ON THE FLOOR WITH HIS FOOT)

GM (TO COMMANDER) Beating up an old woman is fuck-all to be proud of.

DANNY But we've every reason to be proud mister Government Minister. (POINTING GUN AT HIM) Because you are now a prisoner of the Irish Republican Army.

North-East Rap

Irene Tavendale

Hey yoos eens let's move vibrate.
Get i mealie puddins on a plate.
Wir des-pir-it tae hae wir mince.
So ging for it quines,
Dinna sit on i fince.
Move yer bodies, let 'em swing.
Dish 'at tatties wi a fling.
A dollop fir Jimmy, a suppie fir Jock,
Watch 'at loons they're ready tae flock
Aroon yi babe kis yir a dab han'
'at cookin the neeps - by nae means blan'.
Fou o' flavour they will be
A taste tae savour fir you 'n me.
Honky Tonk tatties, Honky Tonk skirlie,
Let's ging baby fir a birlie,
Roon i kitchie
Hey let's move.
At's i stuff wir in i groove.
Jings 'at feed's fair got me jivin.
Fit aboot you?
Are you conivin,
Tae hae yir wicked wye wi me.
Och, onythin ye like - It's po-et-ree!

extract from a novel ....
Heads Above Water
Bill Sluyter

Chapter 1
It's The Way You Tell Them

The office of Blackmountain Retreat Alcoholic Rehabilitation Centre was a cross between a rabbit hutch and a Nissen hut; palatial it was not. A clock ticked away the minutes and three staff members sat mute and in repose.

"I still think that if an alcoholic goes out with ten pounds and comes back sober we're on the right track," said Joanne Reynolds, a petite English brunette with a gamin appearance and a distinct resemblance to the late film actress, Jean Seberg.

Key worker, Ronnie Young, looked over the top of his spectacles, picked up a pencil and tapped his desk with it. "That's okay as far as the Donside and Holburn Homes in Aberdeen are concerned but out here we're comparatively isolated. Anybody can stay sober here. How do we prepare them for life outside?" he asked.

Joanne sat with her arms folded. She looked more like a resident than a staff member, her dark blue cardigan holey at the elbows, jeans frayed at the bottoms. "What do you think, Willie?" She asked, frowning slightly.

Willie James slowly lit a cigarette. "I tend to side with you. Let's take a chance."

"You would say that," said Young, "but you're only doing so to keep in with her."

"Not at all," replied James. "It's my considered opinion. I'd like to try an experiment with Jimmy Jack. Let him loose in Turriff one day with a few bob in his pocket and see what happens."

"Shite," snorted Young. "Liberal crap. Ten to one he'll come back guttered."

Joanna's eyelids flickered. "How do you know that? Each alcoholic is an individual as you're so fond of telling us. From where I see it Jimmy's ready for a day out on his own. I'm impressed by his progress."

Young trapped his pencil on the desk again and a wan smile appeared on his face. "It won't work, Joanna, you're wrong on this one."

"C'mon, its worth a go," said James, absent-mindedly offering Joanna a cigarette which she politely refused.

Joanna stood up and walked across to where the typewriter sat. She idly fiddled with the keys. "Does he have to know?" she asked inquisitively.

"Eric knows if one of us here farts," said Young irreverently.

"Considering the amount of baked beans we get it's highly bloody likely," said James.

Joanna grinned. "Here," she said enthusiastically, "I've got a story for you two. There's this baby just been born and he's grinning from ear to ear. The obstetrician is puzzled and examines the baby. He finds that a tiny fist is clenched and the baby is grinning more than ever. He prizes open the little fingers and what do you think he finds?"

The men exchange glances.

"No idea," said James, "tell us, what did he find?"

"The pill."

Young shook his head. "It's the way you tell 'em," he said.

Chapter 2
TO THE NORTH OF BENNACHIE

No one knows how Blackmountain Retreat got the name. The establishment is surrounded by soft rolling agrarian Aberdeenshire hills where splurges of oilseed rape stand out like yellow oases in seas of green. On the south western horizon lurks dark Bennachie, the craggy Mither Tap a granite reminder of harsher times.

The Blackmountain Superintendent, Eric Stewart, mixes tales of local folklore with dashes of facts served up like a soft drink in a glass of gin. A Baptist, Stewart is inclined to be economical with the truth more often than you would imagine a religious man to be. Most of the residents when confronted by a Stewart anecdote simply shrug shoulders and stoically say: "That's Eric for you".

To his credit, some say, Stewart believes that the only cure for alcoholism is to turn to God. Some residents find this difficult to swallow having forced over their throats all sorts of weird concoctions. Stewart is not over fond of secular cliches but a "natural high" would appear to be his tenet.

Originally a Church of Scotland Home, Blackmountain was converted by Stewart to suit the needs of alcoholics in 1984 and since then it has become a safe enclave for problem drinkers nationwide. A miniature United States, drinkers of all creeds and careers have found solace there.

Intended at the beginning to house men only, modifications were made in late 1988 and women allowed to enter the holy of holies. Joanna had expressed reservations because she thought it would lead to tensions, sexual and otherwise. Young and James too were none too keen on the idea when it was first mooted but time has a habit of dulling incisiveness.

A recreation room was donated by an old company but the pool table looks as if it was found in a skip and the cues and dart board likewise. The kitchen and office are prefabricated buildings and are due to be replaced at a later date. Schemes or scams are thought up now and again to help raise funds for new headquarters and kitchen. Bennachie was climbed by a few of the more agile residents and the princely sum of £107.61 raised. As Joanna succinctly said at the time, "It's just as well the Lord is patient."

Chapter 3

"WHAT'S FOR DINNER?"

Maggie Kynoch the cook was scraping carrots but her mind was elsewhere. She hardly noticed Jackie McInnes, her new kitchen assistant wash the pantry floor. Maggie was convinced husband Jim was having an affair in Aberdeen. A keep fit enthusiast, recently he claimed he was too tired to perform cunnilingus on her. Bastard, she thought, I'll bet he's licking some other cunt. McInnes, whose first day of duty this was, announced he had finished.

"What?" said Maggie.

"The floor. It's done."

"Aye, okay. After ye've washed yer hands ye can make us a cup of tea."

"Fine. Where's the tea an' things?"

She nodded in the direction of the kettle. "Behind there," she said.

McInnes smiled at her. After a peripatetic life of sleeping rough and vomiting in dosshouses it was quite a novelty to wake up in the same bed for two consecutive nights. Some arse on her, he thought but I'm still a bit shaky, not got it together yet. The screwing can wait. McInnes, for a dipsomaniac had an extraordinary high opinion of himself and his sexual capabilities.

She completed her carrot grating, smiled back at him and checked on the soup. Wonder if he's got any more life in him than the last dormant bloke she mused.

Suddenly Stewart burst in like a cyclone in Bangladesh, all arms and legs the epitome of perpetual motion.

"What's for dinner?" he asked, anxious and nervy, portraying all the traits of his servile residents. He was drunk on religion.

"The same as ony ither Tuesday," Maggie answered matter-of-factly, "broth an' mince an' tatties an' carrots."

She grinned inanely at him. Surely he must know by this time the menu seldom varied from week to week.

"That's good, Maggie. Fine. Norma will be here today but not Mark," Stewart said, motioning as if to move in one direction but actually moving in another. Then he left as suddenly as he'd arrived.

She nodded benignly to herself. Not his wife Norma. Fuck's sake. Shrew of a woman. As for his son Mark, nark more like.

McInnes said the tea was ready and did she take sugar. Yes she said one spoon no milk. What's your cup? That one the one with the pussy on it.

He licked his lower lip expectantly.

The broth started to boil over. "Turn doon 'at grill," commanded Maggie.

"Which one?"

"The one with the pan of broth on it."

He was still thinking about her pussy and imagined a luxuriant growth of pubic hair. His penis twitched.

At the kitchen door a face appeared. A careworn face, a face somehow older than the body. It was Alice Cairns, one of the two women residents.

"Hi, Maggie. Want a hand?"

Maggie took a quick sip of tea. "No, it's okay Alice. I've got a new helper." She looked witheringly at McInnes.

McInnes and Alice exchanged pleasantries. If he'd been wearing a tie he'd have straightened it.

"Haven't seen you before," he said.

Alice leaned against the kitchen door. "That's possibly because I'm not long back from Aberdeen. I've had to sort out some family problems, but I've been here about thirteen weeks altogether. My brother Bill is in here too. Know him?"

"Bill Cairns? Aye, I've met him. Quiet sort of guy. Are you? Quiet I mean?"

"Only in my depressed moments. Ask Maggie, she'll tell you all about me."

With that Alice twirled and left.

McInnes was impressed. Women always created a favourable impression on him. On seeing his first photograph of Bessie Braddock he declared she was alluring.

The soup was now bubbling contentedly.

"She seems nice," he said looking at it.

"She is. Hid a hard time in the past. Drugs as well as drink. One thing led ti anither. Ye ken yersel'," said Maggie.

McInnes did and said so.

"Ye'd better awa' through an' get the dinin' tables ready. Save ye fae rushin' later on," Maggie said glancing at the clock.

McInnes, armed with a large tray-like receptacle full of knives, forks and spoons obeyed orders. It would soon be time for the hordes to arrive for dinner. Plus Norma. Maggie groaned internally and checked the soup again.

In the afternoon, when the suckling pig and waffles had time to slide down the gullets, two o'clock rolled around and the residents reluctantly busied themselves for an alcohol meeting. They were divided into three groups. Joanna and Alice and Lisse Fletcher, the other woman in Blackmountain under her wing. One of the men was invited to join but none of them accepted the offer which surprised Joanna as normally they fell over themselves to be part of her group. The meeting was held in the women's dormitory, a small utilitarian building situated as far away from the male one as was practicable.

"Well girls," began Joanna, armed as usual with copious notes, most of which bore no relation to the needs of alcoholics, spiritual or worldly. "Have either of you given any serious thought about what's going to happen to you after you leave here? Considering that your chance of a halfway house for women is next to zero." she continued.

"I suppose," said Lisse, a twenty-eight year old Mancunian, "I'll probably go back to Torry to live with my boyfriend. He's coming up at the weekend to see me. Things will be thrashed out then."

Joanna stole a quick look at some notes.

"How about work?" she asked. "I think it's important you occupy yourselves. Working in a bar is, Lisse, if you don't mind me saying so, not a very good idea."

Lisse grinned at Alice, then shrugged her shoulders. Alice gave a cigarette to her and both women smoked with an air of anxiousness. "You could be right. I don't know, it's difficult. I'm not the type who's suited to a nine to five routine," said Lisse.

"It's in your best interests if you were. We've talked before about how important it is to reject your former way of life. You've got to admit, Lisse, you lack self discipline," said Joanna.

Lisse bit her lower lip. "Point taken, miss."

"There you go again. Why do you think I'm lecturing you?"

"Because you are."

"No. The blinkers have to come off, Lisse."

Alice puckered her mouth and attempted to blow smoke rings. "She's right enough Lisse. We're our worst enemies. You know the story about the well balanced Scot?"

"No" said Lisse, "enlighten me."

"He's got a chip on both shoulders," said Alice.

"How clever. One flaw, Watson. I'm English," retorted Lisse.

Joanna smiled at Alice. "Maybe that's why you're reluctant to accept things, Lisse," she said and looked at the notes again.

"Look, smart arse, I'd be unhappy if I lived on Jupiter. I came here to get help for a drink problem, so how about some help? Scoring points off me doesn't prove anything."

They sat in silence for a few minutes digesting what Lisse had said.

"How about you Alice? You feeling more able to cope with the outside world now?" asked Joanna once the reverie was over.

Alice stubbed her cigarette. "Yes, I've had time here to ponder, get my head together. I'm quietly confident I'll make it this time."

"Good for you," said Joanna.

Lisse stuck out her tongue at them and blew smoke in Joanna's direction.

"Let's continue this tomorrow," she said, "you're not going to believe this but I've got a headache."

Alice and Joanna did believe and class was dismissed.

In a small room adjacent to the office and known euphemistically as 'The Quiet Room', James was holding forth with McInnes, Liverpudlian John Davis and Jimmy Jack from Fraserburgh. They were listening to a tape about the physical effects of alcohol.

"What's the point?" asked Davis a highly strung pessimist, "we know all about this."

"No harm in listening," said James, "we might learn something."

McInnes was day-dreaming, thinking lecherous thoughts about Maggie. Jack, who had never really considered himself an alcoholic, said, "I've never hid ony o' this problems in the mornin'. Oh aye, hangovers, but they passed okay efter a snifter."

James pressed the pause button. "Now lads, any constructive thoughts?"

The men looked glumly at each other.

"No," said Davis with an air of finality.

"Okay, have it your way," said James, "soon be three o'clock anyway. We'll try again on Thursday. Remember to bring your notebooks next time."

"Yes sir," said Davis saluting him.

"Dinna' ken aboot you guys, but I've got grass to cut," said Jack.

McInnes and Davis cursed his enthusiasm.

On Turriff golf course Stewart was playing as well as he had done for weeks. The turf was springy, the birds twittered and all was right with the world as long as the sun shone and the occasionally birdie putt dropped. He was glad to be away from Blackmountain and the mounting machinations.

Corncrake

George Gunn

From the wet corner of a field at the end of June
I would hear your rattle twist calling out
through the green hay crop to your rival
or your mate, unseen, always unseen
although the once I did see you I laughed
at your resemblance to my mother's scrubbing brush
sweet ugly bird, are you thirsty, corncrake
since you have flown over the Sahara Desert
to get here, to this Caithness croft park
how welcome you are, how annoying
'If I see they hoors I'll shoot thum!' my father
rasped, semmit clad in the Simmer Dim at 3 a.m.
but what care you or I for that, bird & boy
each in their wet corner, awake & noisy.

Badenoine

(for Ian Begg)

George Gunn

A man at a threshing mill, his hands
around a sack, the dry sea rattle of grain
into the jute, the yellow sheaves
forked in at the front, important work this

then the harvest was done, the months like clouds
passed, he came back
he always stood here, lighting his twist
one day he wrote on the pine planked sackend

'John Begg, February 13, 1868
A cauld sna. Nae wark the day'
at the steading end, warm in the memory
of harvests past, at the head of Glenbuchat

perhaps the frost relented & he went to the field
perhaps he felt reborn as he approached the plough

The Spaewifie
Charles W Brown

A hid got a fee in a toon near the Brae
Far A chauved wi' ma horse an' ploo a' day
Ma rigs war as snod as the stanes wad alloo
Sae A pleased aul' Hillie o' Wasterloo.

Man aye, it twal powen a term it wis a sair fecht. Bit Hillie wis a
mannie 'it kint a guid warker. He aye pit himsel' aboot tae obleege
me, gin 'ere wis onything A nidded. 'At's foo A got aff till Aikey Fair. The
coorse wither hid cad's a' ahin' wi' wir wark, an' A didna min' pittin' in a
puckly extra oors for the mannie at nicht. Na. A'm nae sae blate! A ken the
wye tae get butter on ma breed. Sae here wis me wi' a day aff, an' fower bob
forby in ma pooch. "Dinna get ower foo!" Hillie warnt. A hid nae sic
intintion. A wis efter Muggie Pittendreich an' noo wis ma chunce tae im-
press her. A hid sillar in ma pooch. Och aye!

Ae eer fan the wither pit's ahin' wi' the hey
A warked it nicht an' A got mair pey
A chunce A thocht tae kittle up ma quine
Sae a took 'er till the Brae till mak her mine.

Muggie didna' tell her mither she wis gyan wi' me, else she widna' hae
got. Noo dinna get me wrang! A wisna the stag bull o' the Howe. Ca'
Jimmy McTupp 'at gin ye like, nae me. A wis canny. It wis jist it 'at time a'
mithers war feert for their lassies.

A wited oot o' sicht o' Muggie's hoose, sittin' on a stane dyke wi' ma
bike plunkit in the girss aside me. It wis twal er she cam pechin' up. She'd
bin hinnert wi' the washin' up, cause her faither hid taen a' the het watter
fae the kettle on the swingle tae sort oot an ailin' soo. Bit 'at wis a' by, sae we
got yokit.

Fit fine it wis tae be in love! A let Muggie gyang in front sae's A could see
mair o' 'er. A wis aye hopin' for a bluffert o' win' sae's A could see still mair
o' 'er. The sax mile wis far ower short. As we cam nearhan' the Brae the

steer gat war an' war. The warstle tae get in aboot! Something awfa! An' the din wis terrible, but fan A think on't noo, it wis a guidnatert din. Chiels shoutin' tae een anither. "Aye, aye min. Foo are ye? Still wi' Bunkie? Nae mairrit yet?"

Abeen a' the spikin', the roarin' o' the traivelin' fowk, ('at's fat they ca' them nooadays), the hurdie gurdie churnin' oot its tinny music, the creak creak o' the showdin' boats and the screechin' o' the quines inside 'im garrin ye think they war feert bit a' the time jist wintin' tae attract the loons.

Muggie took tilt like a duik till watter. She wintit tae try her han' at athing, me peyin' of coorse. A wint on till the showdin' boats wi' her tae begin wi', mair tae get a guid look at her legs gin onything else. Man she wis a topper! A pit her on till the furly-gigs hersel. A hid a gran' view doon below. She wired in till toffee aipples an' the like. She wis fair enjoyin' hersel'.

> The showdies an' the furlers fair took Meg's fancy
> She hurled in 'em a', bit they looked gey chancy
> The floss an' the aipple made a soss o' her claes
> Aikey is gey sair fan the chiel aye peys.

Bit fate in the shape o' a spaewifie took a han' in things. Muggie wid hae her fortune read. 'At aul' besom wi' her gless ballie! "I see you, dressed in flowing white robes, entering an ornate doorway, into a shining white residence. It could be a palace."

Muggie wis dumfoonert. As the wifie wint on, A began tae see ma lass in a new licht. An' war. She gid me a queer look fan she cam oot o' the tint, a kin' o' a doon the nose look, gin ye ken fat a mean. The feel thocht she wis gyan tae mairry a prince, nae doot.

The rest o' the day wis a skunner. A' the wye hame, a' 'at she could spik o' wis o' gettin' a job at the big hoose. Her last wirds wis 'at she widna likely be seein' me again. Weemin! A learnt a lot aboot weemin at Aikey 'at day.

Och aye, a lot o' watter his gid aneth the brig sin then. A've warslet awa' an' deen a' richt for masel, bit mony at time fan A pass the Brae A min' aboot the spaewifie an' her cantrips.

Fit aboot Maggie? Oh, she got an earl a' richt, bit A dinna think it was titled. For a' 'at, A heard it wis a richt bonnie bairn. Eftert, she gid a' tae pot wi' releegion. The puir quine deet wi' cancer nae lang syne.

Mercy me! A've jist hin a thocht! The spaewifie wis richt! She'd bin spikin' aboot Maggie gyan throw the Pearly Gates! Jist as weel 'at Muggie didna ken at the time, puir sowel!

> Noo A'm gyan back tae the Brae eence again
> Wi' sillar in ma pooch 'at A winna spen'
> Muggie'll be watchin' fae the cloods up abeen
> An' minin' on wir day on the Brae lang seen.

Tune:
d d d m m s s s l s m
m m f f f r r m m d
d d m m m s s s l s m
m m f f r r s d d d
(Vary number of notes to suit words)

Do I Belong?

Jean Tarras

What is this North East neuk to which I come?
A stranger, yet with my roots here.
Its blood flows in me; my parents left, but I return.
A stranger, yet I belong.

The bleak landscape in March, endless days of June.
A huge basin of sky above me,
A chill in the air.
A stranger with an English tongue.

Rocky shores and sandy beaches, hills and mountains.
Villages perched on cliff tops, precarious but safe.
Graveyards of my ancestors.
Am I a stranger, or do I belong?

The Day of the Roup
Jean Tarras

George stood leaning on the gate, arms folded on the crossbar. He was gazing at the newly ploughed field. Ploughed but not planted. The fencing was in good order, he noted. Good fencing meant a well kept farm. He was fortunate he could afford new fencing now. In the old days it had been different; patching with old wire, replacing only the most rotten posts. All he could afford in those days.

He shifted his shoulders under his Sunday suit, and glanced down at his muddy shoes. Maggie wouldn't like mud on the carpets. Not that it mattered. Maggie was in hospital and when she came home next week it wouldn't be to the farm but to the retirement house which they had bought in the neighbouring town.

He glanced to his left where the farm implements stood in rows in the park awaiting their turn to be sold tomorrow. Everything was in order. Small items in lots in the big steading, cattle and sheep penned inside. The furniture they did not require in another steading. A place marked out for the teas and another for the bar. An office for the auctioneers in the kitchen. Yes, all was ready for tomorrow.

With a sigh he turned and went towards the house. It needed doing up, he thought critically. It was old fashioned, no central heating even. But the new owners were ready to do all that. Any spare money had gone into the buildings, the land and the livestock in his day.

Maggie hadn't complained. She had worked with him for thirty years to build up a solid, profit making farm. Now they had sold for a good price and Maggie would have all the luxuries she'd never had before. Central heating, double glazing, fitted carpets, a shower in the bathroom and the kitchen of her dreams.

They'd never had children so there was no-one to pass all this on to. They had been sorry about it but thirty years ago you had children or you didn't. You didn't enquire into the why like you did nowadays. Anyway there hadn't been time to bother about it. If there had been silent tears they had remained hidden.

He changed his clothes in the bedroom and gazed out of the window at the rolling acres and the clear sky which betokened frost during the night. It was a hard place, he thought. Generations of people had worked and even died to wrest this fertile land from heather and scrub. Folk looking at the cattle and crops now did not see the hardship which had made the farm land of Aberdeenshire what it was.

He put on his wellies in the lobby and wondered at the bureaucracy which was laying down rules to take that hard won fertility out of use. Set aside. Could you set aside generations of work with the stroke of a pen? It seemed you could.

The cattle court was warm with the breath of the stirks misting the air. Moss, his collie, rose from his bed of straw and looked up at George.

"Aye, Moss, you don't understand, do you?" He bent and patted the dog. "You've no need to worry though. Bert Murray's taking you. There's no way I'd let you be sold to the highest bidder, you're a good worker and you'll get a decent home with Bert."

The dog barked and George heard the outside telephone bell ring. Well he wasn't answering it, it would just be someone asking something about tomorrow.

The cattle looked well. He cast a critical eye over them. They should fetch a fair bit.

He passed through the byre where the milk cow would have been tied. She had already gone. Not many farmers kept a cow these days. Mostly the milk was delivered at the end of the farm road, but Maggie liked to make butter and cheese. He wondered if she would miss all the work or would revel in her freedom? He pushed to the back of his mind the thought of all that free time. It frightened him a bit.

Anyway, Daisy, the cow had gone to a new home a week ago. The milk cow was different from the stirks. It wasn't worth a machine for one cow, and if you'd sat with your head pressed to her warm flank twice a day for years, and felt your hands coax the frothing milk into the bucket, you had a relationship that was special.

The sheep were penned in the near empty hay store. Ewes and lambs and the two rams separately. There were still a few bales of hay and the lambs were playing. Racing up and down, hiding behind bales and jumping out at their comrades. The ewes sat and watched their offspring tolerantly. George smiled and then laughed aloud as a particularly adventurous lamb leapt onto a high bale and stood surveying the others with a supercilious look.

"Right King of the Castle," George murmured.

Time wasters they were, lambs. Somehow you couldn't resist stopping and watching them.

All was well with the stock. He'd go and boil himself an egg and light the fire. He'd had a good dinner in Aberdeen before he'd visited Maggie. She was looking well today. He missed her so much. She would have had the room warm and a fine supper ready for him. This wasn't home without Maggie. He'd be glad when he was out of here.

He put the pan of water on to boil and bread in the toaster. He'd make sure that the new house was warm for Maggie coming home. That time clock for the heating looked a bit complicated but he'd work it out somehow. Tomorrow. He wasn't going to enjoy tomorrow but he'd get through it. He'd been to numerous roups and he'd seen the pain in the other farmers eyes as stock and implements went under the hammer. The breaking up of a life was not easy to bear.

The fire was beginning to burn up. He went to the cupboard and poured himself a dram. He reckoned he deserved it tonight.

The telephone rang but he ignored it as he took the first sip of whisky. It rang and rang until in exasperation he picked it up and said, "Hello," sharply.

Minutes passed as he stood and listened, then he said, "Thank you," and put the receiver down carefully as if it might break.

He sank into his chair before the fire, his face blank and uncomprehending. It must be wrong, it had to be wrong. He did not believe it. He put the whisky glass down and the fireguard on the fire, switched off the cooker and fetched the car keys.

The hospital was quiet, the ward lights dim when he arrived. The nurse and the doctor were kind, but their explanations meant nothing to him.

Maggie was dead.

They let him see her. His Maggie, so cheerful this afternoon, looking forward to her new home and her central heating. Now so still, so young, her face wiped clear of lines, the young girl he had married all those years ago, the girl who had walked side by side with him through good and bad.

He didn't remember driving home but he must have done so for the fire was still in when he got back. He fed it lumps of coal and went out to the steading.

Moss greeted him with a quiet bark and he brought the dog back with him to the house.

He sank into his chair and his hands grasped the dog's thick hair. His head fell forward and he sobbed as he hadn't done since he was six years old.

He awoke shivering as Moss licked his face. A glance at the clock told him that it was 6 am. Why was he here instead of in his bed with the alarm clock sounding? Memory flooded back.

Maggie was gone and it was the day of the roup. The roup must go ahead, he decided. No-one must know until it was all over. With any luck he would be so busy that he wouldn't have time to think.

He let Moss out and took a quick look at the stock. All was well there. He forked over the straw and fed hay and cake to the stirks and sheep.

Back in the house he ran a hot bath, blessing the immersion heater which he had had installed. Dressing in clean clothes he wished he could stop shivering. He had never felt cold like this before, his bones were like ice. A cup of tea didn't help and in desperation he poured whisky into the second cup. Whisky could cure most things, he thought. Many's the lamb he'd saved with a drop when it had arrived on a cold wet night, looking more dead than alive.

George was a quiet man, a man respected by his neighbours. Always ready to give a hand if it was needed they turned out in force, anxious to make his roup a success.

The auctioneers were pleased. Things were going for good prices. Not that the prices weren't deserved, for George kept his implements in good order. The drinks at the bar were also going well and many a man bid more than he had intended or went home with something for which he had no need.

"Aye, George, it's a grand roup." John Strachan took his arm. "You'll have a drink with me. I've just bought that tup of yours. If he produces lambs as good as this year's he'll be worth every penny I paid."

"He'll do that, John." George replied. "But I'll have that drink another time, the auctioneers are needing me." He escaped into the house. It was nearly over, he thought, just the furniture now and he didn't need to be there for that. His head was swimming and he felt sick.

The womanfolk were in the kitchen and he made his way to the sitting room and sank into a chair. He wouldn't be missed for ten minutes.

There was a gentle knock on the door and then it swung open to reveal Linda from the farm next door. A plump woman with the rosy face acquired in many hours of outside work, she laid a tray beside him on the table.

"I'll swear you've had nothing to eat, George. You get that down you and you'll feel better. It'll soon be over now, and tomorrow you can go and see Maggie and tell her what a success it was. Have a wee while to yourself."

George looked up at her kindly face and held on to his self control. He would not, could not, break down now. He looked at the tray and then forced himself to swallow a sandwich and drink a cup of tea. Somehow he would make the effort to see this endless day through. Somehow he would manage to preserve his dignity in front of all these people.

He could hear cars starting up and cheerful shouts of farewell from outside. The sale was over and everyone was leaving.

Rising from his chair he looked out of the window and saw a queue waiting to pay the auctioneers.

Linda popped her head round the door.

"We're off George," she said. "We've cleared up and I've left you a casserole in the oven. Mind you eat it, it'll do you good."

"Thanks, Linda. You've been real good. I don't know how I'd have managed without you."

"Och, away." Linda's smile broadened. "That's what friends are for."

At last the place was quiet. The auctioneers were last to go, but eventually even they packed their boxes and paperwork into the car, shook hands, and took themselves off.

George wandered through the steadings. Empty apart from the litter. The straw covered court cold and silent. Even Moss had gone, jumping quite happily into Bert's Land Rover. George shivered and, switching off the lights, he stepped into the yard. The sun had dropped behind the hills and a chill wind had sprung from the west. The farm seemed to shrug and settle itself deeper into the earth from which it had arisen. There was a broodiness in the air, a waiting for birth, or rebirth. Without crops or animals it faded, became colourless, barren, a thing of no value or importance.

George strolled down to the gate and leaned his arms on it as he had done last night. Just one day and the world had turned upside down. There was truly no place for him here now, or perhaps this was the only place for him. He sighed, his far sighted eyes picking out the smoke from the chimney of Linda's farm. The rooks were going in to roost, the starlings scattering about the steading. The mournful hoot of an owl echoed over the fields. Here and there an implement thrust its shadow against the sky. Waiting to be collected by its new owner, it gave the impression of modern sculpture in an alien landscape.

George turned and looked towards the house. A light shone in the kitchen window, otherwise it was dark. A square shadow sitting in its small square garden where Maggie had grown her lilies and marigolds.

Maggie....oh......Maggie. It was as though with her passing death had spread its mantle over all. It was right that it should be so for Maggie had been the light of the place. The moving spirit; like the engine of the carousel which switched on the lights, played the music and set the horses gliding up and down on their poles.

There was a field, a small and secluded field to the south of the house. This had been Maggie's favourite place. It was here that she had fed the orphan lambs. They had rushed to the gate as soon as they heard her approaching and George would stop his work and smile as he watched them wagging their tails as they sucked furiously at the bottles. On warm summer evenings a walk around the small field had become a benison before a last cup of tea and bed.

They had walked hand in hand, sure of their privacy, and content in themselves.

George opened the gate and wandered over the spring grass. Damp with dew, his footsteps left green depressions as he went. He wondered if he could go on, he was so tired and cold. Yet he felt close to Maggie here: he stretched out a hand and almost, almost, she took hold.

He took a deep breath and a pain shot through his chest and down his arm.

He called her name and she answered him.

The Pressed Leaf

Ian Crockatt

The leaf lay on the page,
sapless, flat,
killed not by age
but being picked and crushed; just that.

I touched the squashed veins
and splayed stem
which cool rain
had once made round and useful; and loved them,

and championed them in words,
wild - but look -
pressed, prematurely lifeless, hardly heard,
in a book.

A book which was a tree, minted
in pure rage,
now chopped, planked, pulped and printed;
page by page.

And I, on each white page,
sapless, flat,
crushed not by rage
but making words of it; just that.

Pastoral

Henry Adam

Mobil

joint winner of
1994 MOBIL
SCOTTISH
PLAYWRIGHTS'
COMPETITION

SYNOPSIS

The play begins with the fevered dream of David Gordon. He dreams that he is trying to get home but can't. He wakes screaming. It is the beginning of 1946. He has returned from the war to his family's farm in Kincardine on the verge of mental and physical collapse. Although a journalist by trade, he has set his mind on the farm, on returning to the land to rejuvenate himself. In this he is almost successful, but a land dispute - a Polish family has moved on to land his future brother-in-law was "promised" - erupts into violence, reminding him too closely of the carnage he thought he'd left behind. A friendship develops between David and Anna, the eldest daughter of the Polish family, much to the disapproval of his mother, sister and future brother-in-law. The following is the second scene of act II.

ACT 2
SCENE II

THE HILLSIDE. DARKNESS. DAVID AND ANNA SIT TOGETHER.
ANNA The nights can be so beautiful. It's frightening. Why is it so still and calm? Do you think the trees know that we are here? We should thank them, thank them for watching over us. And that bird ... the one that sings ... (PAUSE) I saw you working today. Up on the hill, overlooking our land.

DAVID You should've come up.

ANNA That man was there. The one who will marry your sister. (PAUSE) Anyway, why look for trouble. Your mother has already taken against me. (PAUSE) Were you working hard?

DAVID Hard enough. A dinna mind

ANNA No, work suits you. You are growing strong.

DAVID A wis aye strong.

ANNA Were you? Yes, I think perhaps you were. I don't know why I thought you were an invalid. Perhaps it was just the gunshot wound.

DAVID (Flexing arm) Good as new.

ANNA Good. It's good that you heal quickly. (SHE PLAYS WITH HIS HAND) What happened to your hand ... it's covered in cuts ..?

DAVID Pykit weer. (Seeing she

doesn't understand) Barbed wire.
We've been pitting up barbed wire.
A'm an expert now on barbed
wire. A'll write a thesis on it
someday,

ANNA (Smiling) I forget you are an
intellectual. You don't look the
part.

DAVID Jaist a bothy loon, eh?

ANNA A boothy loon. Someday
you should come round and I'll
teach you English. I don't know
what my English teacher would
make of you.

DAVID Bottom o ae class.
Stannin in ae coarner wi a dunce's
cup.

ANNA Yes. That would be you.
So ... what would you say, in this
thesis on barbed wire?

DAVID God knows. Why say
anything.

ANNA Maybe you have a duty.

DAVID What duty?

ANNA All educated men have a
duty. It's like being a soldier.

DAVID A've deserted

ANNA You're a funny boy. I
don't know why you are here.

DAVID I'm not a boy.

ANNA Aren't you? Maybe not.
I look at you and see a boy. Why
are you here David? Why are your
hands covered in callouses and
cuts? A million people could fix
that fence. Five million. Ten
million.

DAVID It's my land, or rather
it'll be my land. A man should
fix his ain finces.

ANNA And how high will you
build them?

DAVID High enough.

ANNA It's funny ... a man like
you, a place like this ... it's a puzzle.

DAVID Is it?

ANNA Yes

DAVID A wis sent away fae here,
ye know. A wis a fairmer an they
sent me awye. Fin a came back a
wis a student ... a student o history
... o architecture ... a kint aboot
literature ... everything great an
good. An a loved it. For a while
a really loved it. Ae whole history
o civilisation wis in ma hiyd, an a
kipt it ere, safe, secure. A kint if
ae hale warld wis tae disappear
tomorrow a new generation could
build it up again fae ae things it
were stored in ma hiyd. A kint ae
pattern, see. A understood.
Everything, everything wis flowin
in ae same direction - every book,
every building, every religion,
every science ... everything that
man bed ever made wis workin
towards ae same goal. We were
building a mirror, a mirror in
which mankind could see its ain
face. On ae 5th o May, 1945, we
found at mirror, me an some loons
no unlek masel. We stood on ae
brink an looked intae ae face o
man. For ae first time in ae
history o ae warld, we found oot
fit we were capable o. A looked
intae at mirror an a saw ma ain
face ... I saw ma face ... There's
nithing quite as ugly as ae face o a
man. D'ye wint tae ken why a'm
here Anna? A'm here because a

wis there. Because a wis there
a'm here. A lek it here, Anna ...
a lek it here.

ANNA Sssh David ... the war's
over.

DAVID No. At's far a'body's
wrong. The war isna over. It's
still going on. It's in a' o us ... a'
o us!

ANNA Don't talk about it.

DAVID It's true. It's true. Ae
idea it fit isna white is dirty didna
start wi ae Nazi's, it willna end wi
them either. It's in a' o us. Even
oor bairns.

ANNA (Inducing David to sit) It's
wrong for a boy to know so much.

DAVID A'm no a boy. Anna ...

ANNA Uh-huh ...

DAVID Why d'ye no wear yer
wedding ring?

ANNA (After pause) You noticed? I
didn't think you were so
perceptive.

DAVID It wisna me ... ma
mither, she noticed..

ANNA Your mother. Yes.

DAVID She thinks it's sinful,
me galavantin wi a mairriet
wumman.

ANNA And what do you think?

DAVID I think it's nane o ma
mither's business.

ANNA What's she like, your
mother?

DAVID Hard.

ANNA In what way?

DAVID In ae way a stone is hard. A canna mind ae last kind word she said tae me.

ANNA I'm sure a man like you would have no difficulty finding someone to offer a kind word.

DAVID Anna? Why don't ye wear it?

ANNA Do you mourn your dead, David?

DAVID Aye, ye know a do.

ANNA Yes. You mourn in your own way. Quietly. When so many are dead it's best not to make a fuss.

DAVID He's dead then?

ANNA They're never quite dead, are they? No one really dies. Even when you can't remember any more, you never quite forget. The dead turn to mist. They band together and dance in front of your eyes. After the first you can never see clearly. When there are enough you can't see at all. The world now is populated by the blind. You know how blind we are David? We sit so close together and yet we can't see each other. All we see is the mist, and the vague outline of a hand, reaching … Here, give me your hand. That's better. Do you think the moon will go behind that cloud soon?

DAVID A dinna ken. D'ye want it to?

ANNA Yes. It never quite gets

dark enough here, does it?

DAVID In ae winter. In ae winter it does.

ANNA (GETS UP AND LOOKS AROUND HER)

DAVID D'ye lek ae darkness?

ANNA Have you ever met a blind man David? When you meet a blind man he puts his hand to your face. (SHE PUTS HER PALM ON DAVID'S CHEEK) In this way he gets to know you. (She searches his face with her hand) He asks no questions, makes no assumptions … he sees more thoroughly, in darkness … silence. Close your eyes. Don't talk. Words are for the living, the clear-sighted. Give me your hand. (SHE PLACES HIS HAND ON HER CHEEK) Can you see me? Can you see me?

DAVID (WHISPERED) Anna..

ANNA No, not Anna. Can you see me?

DAVID (LAUGHING) A canna see a thing.

ANNA (LAUGHING WITH HIM) You look nice when you laugh … your face looks nice. Why is your smile so gentle, 1 wonder … your eyes so soft and your hands so hard? Have you ever loved anyone David? No? But you've been kind, tender … how long ago, I wonder, since you did not love, but were kind, tender. I'm glad I met you, you know? I thought life from now on would be lonely, but not … I would like it, you know, if you did not love me, but were kind … tender … (SHE HAS MANIPULATED HIS HAND ONTO HER BREAST) Don't stop, what's wrong?

DAVID Your skin's so soft..

ANNA Yes … close your eyes. This is how the blind see, the dumb talk..

DAVID Who was he?

ANNA Don't talk.

DAVID Anna. Who was he?

ANNA Who?

DAVID Your husband?

ANNA Sssh David..

DAVID Tell me..

ANNA A man. just a man. Any man. You know him. You saw him. If you didn't see him in Krakow then you saw him in Vienna. You saw him in Berlin.

DAVID But …

ANNA Don't talk. Lie back.

DAVID (LIES BACK)

ANNA (UNBUTTONS HIS SHIRT, SHE BEGINS TO KISS HIS STOMACH)

DAVID Did he love you?

ANNA Mmmn …

DAVID Did he love you Anna? Tell me?

ANNA (LOSING PATIENCE) Yes. He loved me. He loved me. The world is full of men who love their wives David. They love them so much and yet they trade them for cigarettes. Do you want a cigarette David? Would you like me to get you some? He loved me. Of course he loved me. He was a man, and like all men, he loved me most

when his penis was in my mouth
... with my cigarettes in his pocket
he loved me.
A LONG SILENCE FALLS BETWEEN THEM. THEY DO
NOT LOOK AT EACH OTHER. ANNA BUTTONS
HERSELF UP.

ANNA You won't ever love me,
will you David.

DAVID No. I promise.

ANNA (CRADLING HIS HEAD AGAINST HER
BELLY) Good. Good.

(THE TWO CONTINUE THEIR RELATIONSHIP
DESPITE PROTESTS. DAVID IS MORE AND MORE
DISTURBED BY WHAT HE HEARS PEOPLE SAYING.
HIS FRIEND TIM, A LABOUR ACTIVIST ON THE
COAST, TRIES TO PERSUADE HIM TO WORK WITH
HIM IN THE CREATION OF A 'NEW JERUSALEM'.
THE IDEA BEGINS TO SOUND APPEALING. THE
FOLLOWING SCENE IS THE EIGHTH OF THE SECOND
ACT.)

SCENE VIII

DAVID AND ANNA ON HILLSIDE. DAYLIGHT.

ANNA You're quiet this morning.

DAVID Am a?

ANNA (STROKING HIS HAIR) Quiet as a
mouse in a house of cats. (IN THE
DISTANCE CHURCHBELLS RING) Listen,
they're going to church.

DAVID All the good Christians.

ANNA All the good Christians,
going to church. It must be good
to be like them, to know so
certainly what's right, what's
wrong ... to think in terms of
good and evil, knowing yourself
to be good, unquestionably good.

DAVID Oh they're good. Any
fool can see at. No, they're good,
They are good. At's why a cam
back, ken ... because they were
'good'. Ye live on good land an
ye eat good food an ye mix wi good
people. Efter a while ye become

good yersel. Efter a while ye lose
yer shame. At least at's ae theory.

ANNA Are you becoming good,
David?
DAVID No, it's jaist a theory.
Ae fevered hypothesis o a sick
mind. Back then though it made
a lot o sinse. Ye leave behind ae
rubble, ae bodies, ae barbed wire.
Ye leave behind ae skies made grey
by ae collective shame o a
continent. Ye travel tae a green
land, wi rich earth an blue skies.
Ye listen tae ae birds sing. Ye
watch ae girss grow. Ye forget. It
gets intae yer hiyd an ye canna let
it go. Ye start tae unnerstan why
ae salmon swim upstream. Going
home. Home. Ye tell yersel sic
stories. Ye re-invent Eden an ye
say, 'At's far a come fae, at's far
a'm gaen.' Ye live on good land
an ye eat good food an ye mix wi
good people. Efter a while ye
become good yersel. Efter a while
ye'll forget. Ye'll start tae grow
again.

ANNA You are growing David.
We both are.

DAVID Are we?

ANNA Yes, I think we are. Do
you trust me David? I trust you.
A month ago I would not have
said that. The thought of it would
not even have entered my head.
It's silly, isn't it? A little thing,
hardly anything, a little sprig from
an olive branch clutched in the
beak of a dove. A month ago I
would not even have thought to
send out that dove. The waters
were so high it seemed pointless.

DAVID It wis.

ANNA (GOING TO TOUCH HIM) No.

DAVID Dinna!

ANNA What is it?

DAVID A've had enough Anna.
A'm through, A'm lavin here
Anna. A'm lavin.

ANNA Just like that?

DAVID Aye. Jaist lek at.

ANNA Where will you go?

DAVID A dinna ken. Montrose
maybe.

ANNA To work with your friend?

DAVID Aye. Why no. There's
things t'dae, warlds tae chinge!

ANNA Men like you, it's easy for
you to change the world. All you
have to do is say 'I'm leaving',
and already the world is changed.
Maybe you should ask first, ask
the people living there if they want
the world to change.

DAVID It wis ye it said it. 'What
am I doing here?' So fit am a daein
here. Livin oot ae dreams o a
tired and scared sodier. Christ, a
year ago a'd've traded onything
jaist tae see is land again. A' a
winted wis tae touch ae earth a
wis boarn tae touch. Bit fit
seemed richt in ae winter o '45
jaist seems lek a joke now. When
a re-invented Eden a forgot one
thing. A forgot ae wye wimmen
listen tae ae hissin o snakes, an
tak them at their ward.

ANNA You're talking about me?

DAVID No, a'm no talkin aboot
ye. A'm talkin aboot ma mither,
a'm talkin aboot ma sister, a'm
talkin aboot a' ae wimmen sittin

in their finery in ae pews o at kirk, an their men it are nae better than wimmen wi their connivin dirty lies.

HE BREAKS OFF.

DAVID Christ Anna, ye dinna ken fit it's lek livin in at hoose. Nithing's ever said. There's nae need tae say it. Ma mither's got is wye of jaist sittin it maks a'thing crystal clear. A never kint fit an eloquent silence wis until a heard ae wards she never actually said, until a felt them crawlin on ma skin lek ae leeches they are, suckin ae blood fae me.

ANNA You've got me.

DAVID Aye, a ken. A widnae've lasted is lang if it hedna been fer ye. But is at enough? Is at enough tae keep me here amongst a' is good people?

ANNA It's enough for me.

PAUSE

DAVID Ken ma sister Keet? She's ae maist precious thing in ae warld tae me. Last wik a slapped her. Slapped her fice. Fit's happenin tae me fin a'm at ae stage far a'm slappin ma ain sister across ae fice?

ANNA Why did you hit her?

DAVID A dinna ken. She said something.

ANNA Something about me?

DAVID Aye, something aboot ye.

ANNA You don't have to defend me David. I don't care what people say about me.

DAVID I care.

ANNA What did she say that was so bad? That my morals were loose? That my family were thieves? That I was foreign? Different from you? Don't pay any attention David. I don't. It's natural. This happens everywhere, all the time you think that because these people are your friends and family they are better than everybody else? More tolerant? Less scared? David, these are simple people. They don't know the world. They live on fenced off pieces of land - fenced off, you understand - they raise cows, sheep ... after a hundred years you get to be like the animals you care for ... it happens among my family as well as yours. They are herd animals, David ... when they are placid they are placid together, when they are scared they are scared together. You raise cattle. You know. If one gets started it spreads, they panic. With sheep even the scent of a dog can set them off. It doesn't matter that the dog is friendly, that it has no teeth, that it is as scared of them as they are of it..

DAVID So you think it's okay?

ANNA No, it's not okay, but it's not unheard of. It's not something to worry about unduly.

DAVID Unduly ... oh Christ, Anna, a'm no worried unduly.

All these good people, off tae ae Kirk in their Sunday best. They're no better than Nazis for Christsake. They're no better than ae cunts it voted for Hitler.

ANNA No ... you are wrong. You don't know David. You never lived with them. You never saw.

DAVID I saw.

ANNA Maybe ... maybe you saw ... we lived with them ... every day for five years we lived.

DAVID A'll tell ye fit else a saw. A saw fit they did tae yer brither yesterday.

ANNA Darius?

DAVID Aye Darius. There were fower o them, jaist layin intae him. He didna hae a chance. It wis me it stopped them. It wis me it took him back tae ae fairm. Me it cleaned him up so his faither widna see him lek at.

ANNA Thank you. Thank you for looking after him.

DAVID Fit else could a dae? Stan aroon an watch lek at crowd in ae village.

ANNA No.

DAVID A took him hame, wiped his face. A said tae him, 'Get in ae truck. Get in ae truck an a'll tak ye hame.' 'Home,' he said. 'Yes, I would like very much if you'd take me home.'

PAUSE

DAVID 'I would like very much if you'd take me home.'

ANNA You're a kind man David. If others are not kind it is not your fault.

DAVID A thocht a'd left all is behind me. A actually thocht a could turn ma back.

ANNA I knew he'd been in a fight. I didn't know four. (PAUSE) Did he say what the fight was about?

DAVID No.

ANNA He's hot-headed my brother. He could have started it himself. I would not put it past him David. You mustn't assume ...

DAVID Four o them. Twice his size.

ANNA You don't know what my brother is like.
DAVID Oh Anna, a ken fit yer brither's lek. A saw him. A wiped ae blood aff his fice. A saw ae look in his eyes fin he said 'Home.'

LONG PAUSE

ANNA Don't go away because of this David. I need you, you know. You're the only friend I have.

DAVID It's no jaist because o is. Is is jaist ae last straw. A wis wrong. Wrong tae come here. Wrong tae leave here in ae first plice. Jaist plain wrong. Ma whole life ... it's jaist wrong.

ANNA And me?

DAVID A do'no.

ANNA Don't go David.

DAVID A've got tae go. A canna stye here.

ANNA I'll miss you.

DAVID Come wi me.

ANNA I'm tired David. My legs are weak. How far do you think I could run? I have my father to think about. Your father too.

DAVID Fit aboot ma faither?

ANNA He's old David. You shouldn't leave him now.

DAVID He's nae at auld.

ANNA A man is old as soon as his thoughts turn inward, as soon as he starts to think only of the past. Haven't you seen him, sitting in silence, smiling to himself? Do you think it's of the future he thinks? Do you think it's the future that makes him smile? Don't go David. Don't go.

ANNA EMBRACES DAVID. HOLDING HIM CLOSE SHE KISSES HIS NECK SLOWLY AND REPEATEDLY, MURMURING 'DON'T GO, DON'T GO'. HER CARESSES FOLLOW A PROGRESSION FROM A NEED FOR COMFORT TO A WILL TO AROUSE.

DAVID Let me be, for Christ's sake. Let me be.

ANNA CONTINUES. DAVID GIVES IN. EVEN WHEN THEY MAKE LOVE HE WHISPERS, 'LET ME BE'.
THAT NIGHT DAVID IS FOUND BY HIS FATHER, STILL AWAKE AT 3 AM, PACING THE FLOOR. HE OFFERS SUPPORT, TRYING TO GET TO THE ROOT OF DAVID'S PROBLEMS. EVENTUALLY DAVID BLURTS IT OUT. THE FOLLOWING IS FROM SCENE NINE OF THE SECOND ACT.

DAVID A dinna ken if ye mind, it wis a while ago noo ... a telt ye aboot a quine a kint ... Yetta ... ae quine wi broon eyes.

ALEX Aye, oot in ae barn.

DAVID Aye ... aye ... a never telt ye ae hale story. Christ, a never telt ye ae half o it. It wis last year ... last May ... a little toon doon aboot ae Czech border. We were sweepin through Europe by then, sweepin through ... we were ae white angel o liberation, everywhere we went there wis flags wavin, fowk cheerin ... then ... then ... Christ, there are no words, no wye o sayin it ... no wye tae describe fit we saw, fit at fowk wint through, withoot feeling lek a fraud, withoot feelin partly tae blame yersel. An yet we've got tae spik aboot it, we've got tae write doon fit we saw. In fifty years time we'll a' be deed an fin we're deed they'll say it never happened, they'll say it wis jaist a lie ... oh Christ min ... Christ ... a wish tae Christ it wis jaist a lie.
It wis jaist a little toon. Ye'd be hard pressed ae find it on a map. jaist a shitty little toon, no different fae ony plice else. First thing we noticed wis ae smell - we didna ken fit it wis - then ae looks on fowks fices - they coudna look us in ae eye. Aboot a mile past we found it. It didna look lek muckle. We thocht at first it wis a barracks ... a POW camp or something. Then we saw ae chimney. Ye've heard aboot ae camps, ye must've done, ae death camps ... ae horror camps. We entered at plice in silence. They stared at us as if we were fae ae moon. They didna see liberation; all they saw wis sodjers, uniforms, guns. Is sodjer, jaist a loon mibbe he didna unnerstan fit he wis seein - he grabbed ine o them an shook him - he shook him, ye coud hear him rattle - an he wis shoutin, 'It's okay, it's okay, we're Americans,

Americans.' 'Americans,' he said, an it wis as if he didna ken fit an American wis. Then it clicked. They were a' aroon us ... jaist skin an bon, lek dancin skeletons ... some fuckin grotesque puppets made fae sticks an glue ... They were dyin lek flies ... stervin ... ae lucky ines ... ae ines it hedna been gassed, ae ines it hedna been turned intae soap bars and lampshades an ... oh Christ min, ther were bodies everywhere, human bodies ... no, they werena human ... they used tae be human, they used tae be happy, smilin people, people wi jobs an clothes an sets o values ... fitever it is it maks fowk human. They used tae be human, they used tae be ... A stood ere, a jaist stood ere ... an in ae midst o a' at a started tae mind something ... something fae years ago ... A wis five years aul an ye'd taken me intae Montrose. Ye hed tae ging in tae Jim Bain, Jim Bain in ae slaughterhouse. Ye took me in, ye held ma haun, a wis pullin, strugglin, greetin ma een oot. 'Feesht,' ye said tae me, 'Feesht, feesht loon, they're only sheep' ... an a walked through at camp, ma stomach turned tae shite, an ower an ower an ower again a said tae masel 'Feesht! Feesht! They're only sheep! They're only sheep! They're only sheep! They're only sheep!'

ALEX Feesht loon, feesh..

DAVID No ... at's no fit a wis gaen tae tell ye. A wis gaen tae tell ye aboot Yetta, Yetta ... ae quine. A found her ere in ine o ae huts. She wis lyin on a bunk too weak tae move. Her mither wis aside her. Her mither wis dead. She wis clingin tae a mither it hed been deed ae best part o a wik. A

thocht she wis deed hersel. There wisna muckle difference atween her an ae ines it were. A turned her ower, jaist on ae off chance. A turned her ower an she opened her eyes. In ae midst o a' at a saw her eyes ... (WITH CRUELTY IN HIS VOICE) Feesht! They're only sheep! They're only sheep! They're only sheep!

BREAKING NEW
GROUND
Alex Smith Prize

Blue Toon Anguish
Michael Ross

B ein' Bunty Ella's Tammy Da'son's Teeny
Strachan's youngest loon I am in the verra
position to tell ye aboot the time Sartre came to Peterheed.
Y'see we didnae ken he wis affa important at a'. The
only sort o' meanin' he had for us folk wis the fact that
Bunty Ella's man, John the Jiner, wis' oot in the trenches
in the First War. He got pally wi' this mannie fa wis' an
uncle o' Sartre's. It wisnae lang afore they got really
friendly and John wis introduced tae Jean Paul Sartre fa'
we ken noo as an intellectual, philosopher, psychologist,
politician and general shit-stirrin' man o' letters. Bit fin
John the Jiner kent him he wis really only starting oot in
the world. A mannie in his twenties. Nae much o'
nithing really.

John the Jiner did really weel efter the War and built
up his business wi' the result that he wis'aboot the only
cheel frae these parts that geid continental holidays.
Ayewis tae France of course. And it turns oot that he wis
real weel thocht o' by this Jean Paul. He wis only the
young mannie and wis apparently pretty impressed wi'
the man o' the world, spik as ye find antics o' oor John.
John wid tak' him oot mony a nicht tae the Brasseries for
a skelp o' drink and they wid get pretty plastered.

Noo accordin' tae your official histories aboot this
Jean Paul Sartre he wis aye a pretty precociously developed
brainy kind o' chap. Bit this is sheer fraudulence. The
media hisnae changed. A' lees. Sartre, if the truth be
told, wisnae jist the full shillin'. Kent foo tae spin a tale
and blether awa wi' high falutin' words he'd picked oot

o' the French equivalent o' the Thesaurus. Bit it wis a' pretty shalla' meaningless sort o' dirt.

Bit oor John hid read a damn lot. We've a damn good library in Peterhead and John hid crammed himsel' full o' history, philosophy and so on. You name it. Fin Bunty Ella hid her wifies frae the Guild in for an evenin' oor John wid stick his heed in a book. Kent fit he wis speakin' aboot. So, onywye, it turned oot that fin Bunty Ella wis awa spennin' a' her siller doon the mair exclusive shoppies in Paris oor John wis ha'in' gye serious spicks wi' Jean Paul or 'Paulie' as the Jiner ca'd him.

Oh aye ... there wis' aye this wifie hinging aboot wi' Paulie, Simone somebody or ither. Never got on affa weel wi' John the Jiner. Felt that he wis commandeerin' too much o' Paulie's time. Jealous sort o' vratch wis foo the Jiner termed her. Later on, years later in fact, Paulie wis aye draggin' roon a gey miserable lookin' soul Albert Camus tae the Brasseries. Bit John didnae think too much o' him either. Tempramental sort o' bugger wis the Jiner's verdict. Aye a bit o' an ootsider.

But I'm gettin' awa frae ma story aboot foo Paulie came tae Peterhead. Well this particular year, 1931, I think it wis, the Jiner took a helluva bad dose o' shingles and he wisnae up tae gan tae Paris that year. So onywye he telegraphed oor Jean Paul and asked him ower tae bide for his holidays in Peterhead.

Weel Paulie wis fair tricked apparently since he wisnae gettin' on affa weel wi' thon Simone wifie ... apparently there wis aye a blow up aboot something. Too much time spent sittin' on their airses speaking a lot o' tripe mair than likely. Onywye oor Paulie wis mair than pleased tae tak' up the Jiner's offer.

That summer Sartre hid spent a day or twa in Edinburgh bit hidnae found the folk affa accomodatin' ava. Ae wifie in a Morningside Bed and Breakfast wisnae exactly chuffed fin she found Paulie bathin' his bare dock in the wash hand basin. Well I mean tae say the French are mair particular aboot hygiene and he'd thocht it wis een o' these things they dicht their privates in like back hame. Bit Paulie should hae kint he widnae hae tae clumb up a' that distance ontae the thing. Guid behear. As though the basin wis dual purpose. As I said, nae quite the full shillin'.

So he didnae hinner in the Capital bit came up tae Aiberdeen where

Bunty Ella met him and drove him oot tae Peterheed. Well apparently that wis an experience in itsel'. Wi' John ha'in the shingles he wisnae fit tae drive and Bunty Ella wisnae fit tae drive at ony time. Paulie was in a state o' considerable shock by the time they drove past the Lido. They hid narrowly missed twa tractors roon twa bends fin Bunty hid the fit doon and a fish larry hid nearly shot aff the road fin she skited the car roon ower quick at anither corner.

Well. That nicht at 'Dinner' ... they hid fair tin on the continental habits ... Paulie wisnae able tae eat a thing. Bunty Ella wis fair poot oot since she hid spent some considerable time preparing Hairy Tatties wi' Garlic and ingins as a special treat for her French guest. But byes the bye John and Paulie hid a chance tae sit and hae a blether ower a brandie or twa.

Now ye hive tae understand the particular circumstances of that evening tae see how earth shatterin'ly significant it turned oot tae be.

Ye hiv twa mannies. Ane wi' a helluva bad dose o' the shingles and the ither hivin' experienced the traumas o' Buntie's drivin'. A mair miserable pair o' buggers would be hard tae find. And of course the drink had definitely not helped.

Noo I got the jist o' a' this episode fae Bunty Ella's servant quine Uggie Buchan fa' wis Jocky Benzie the Slater's ... och I suppose that disane really maitter ... and later on fae John himsel ... So ye hiv tae imagine them sittin' there gey miserable aboot a'thing. Paulie hid started off by saying that he hid never hin an experience like that. He wis very circumspect aboot Bunty's drivin' being the guest and so on, bit plain spickin' John wid hae neen o't. She's a bloody dangerous bitch wis foo he described his ain wife's drivin' tae Paulie.

It wis scarcely surprisin' that Paulie said tae John that it hid a been a terrible experience. It wis the first time he hid faced the fact o' his mortality. In fact wi' Buntie's drivin' he'd hin tae face it three times in thirty or so miles as it turned oot. Well ye hiv' tae laugh. Bein' a fisherman masel' ye dinna need me tae tell ye that mony folk in a' sorts o' jobs face the fact o' their mortality considerably mair often than wir cheel frae the Brasseries o' Gay Paree. Bit that's a fact o' life. It's a sad reflection on oor Paulie that he hidnae gane death much thocht aboot afore. But oor John fae hid been in the Trenches, and, being ever the dry North East diplomat when circumstances demanded or sentiment raised its unwelcome heid, let it slide. He'd get his oar in at some ither time withoot a doot.

Paulie hid fair hin' a fear. That wis the thing. Onywye tae cheer him up John proposed that he tak him doon tae the fishmarket the next mornin'. And so the dawn rose tae find Jean Paul with a considerable hangover and John the Jiner, shingles notwithstanding, gravely discussin' the relative merits o' the various types o' fish that hid been landed that particular mornin'.

As fate would have it oor Paulie had not noticed where he wis pittin' his feet. He skited on a particularly hazardous weet bit o' the harbour and fell flat in amongst a boxfae o' haddock heids.

Fortunately he wisnae hain' tae face the angst o' a near death experience yet again bit there wis nae doot some Road tae Damascus sort o' insight hid revealed itsel' tae oor French chiel.

As he dichted up the mess he hid made o' himsel' in the wifies lavvie, the gents bein' oot o' order, Paulie hid stared at himsel' in the mirror wi' John guardin' the door. The Jiner fair took a fleg fin he noticed, as he put it, Paulie lookin' as though he wis hypnotised like a rabbit by a car's heedlichts.

John, he'd said in his pigeon English. I 'ave had anozer revalation. I'm sickened. Nauseated een fact, he said. Well oor John telt him that he wis scarcely surprised. A moofae of Haddock heid wid pit onybody aff and gaur them cowk.

No ... no ... you don't understand! said oor Paulie. The fact eet was a haddock head een my mouth makes no differonce. Eet was zee experience of being faced with the Absurdity of eet all. The meaningless of zee fish as I gazed at eet. Zee empty look. Eets cold staring eyes. Eets wetness. Eets sheer inappropriateness. My anguish at eets nothingness.

Well! John the Jiner thocht he hid gin his heid a fair dunt and he wis bein' delirious.

But Paulie would have none of it. He hid babbled on aboot anguish, nothingness an absurdity for some considerable time that morning. And John wis fair embarrassed when Jean Paul hid gin past some o' his auld freens in the Longate grinnin' wi' a feel look on his face shoutin' aboot, "Don't you see John? We are all really free! We are all really free!"

And it's a fact that a lot o' Peterhead folk mind to this day the story aboot a feel French mannie shoutin' a lot o' shite doon the toon on that particular morning. Ye see we're nae eesed tae folk bawlin' oot a' their affairs in broad daylicht.

Onywye tae cut a long story short it wisnae lang after that incident that Paulie shot aff hame tae France since he hid been helluva desperate tae jot doon his experiences in the Blue Toon. Well you can imagine that John the Jiner wis somewhat anxious aboot the prospect o' his French buddy writing jist onything aboot the folk o' Peterhead. There wis nae wye that he wid get Bunty tae emigrate tae the Broch or onywye else if Paulie wrote ony scandal and they had tae skedaddle.

As it turned oot naething ever happened. Oor Paulie became famous in later life as we a' ken through his Existentialist philosophy. Fitever that's aboot. Oh aye...apparently in early editions of his works there used tae be a tribute tae "His friends in Peterhead to whom blah blah ... all this would not have been possible blah blah ..."

But it wis a' a mystery. We couldnae see that he hid enjoyed a particularly relaxing holiday which micht hae spurred his creative juices tae lead tae that ringin' endorsement.

It's aye been a bit o' a puzzle.

Changing Faces

Morag Bisset

THE CHARACTERS

DOD STEWART

GRACE STEWART

STUEE STEWART

ALICK STEWART

JESS STEWART

JOHN the butcher

SANDY a farmer

FREDDY a farmer

JEREMY a farmer

SCENE 1

THE PLAY OPENS IN THE KITCHEN WITH GRACE SURROUNDED BY BOXES. SHE IS SAT AT THE TABLE BUSY WRAPPING UP CHINA CUPS IN OLD NEWSPAPERS. THERE IS A KNOCK AT THE DOOR.

JOHN Hello!

GRACE Come in John! (ENTER JOHN) ... I didni hear ye comin' in aboot,

JOHN Fit like i day wifee?

GRACE Och God, dinna ask ... (SHAKING HER HEAD) ... hash't aff mi feet

JOHN I'll say ye are, I better nae pit yer beef doon throu' here. Ye'll mibbee get it tint amongst a' 'es boxes.

GRACE (STANDS UP) see ... (TAKES THE BOX FROM JOHN) I'll pit it throu' in i scullery oot i wye.

JOHN I think I've got athin' ye wis wintin' ... (JOHN CHECKS A LIST) Pun a mince, saasages, bilin' beef, shooder steak, twa meelie jimmies in a couple a packets a Stockins

breid ... I think 'ats aboot yer lottie.

GRACE At soons aboot richt ... foo muckles 'at noo? (GRACE GOES TO THE SIDEBOARD FOR HER PURSE)

JOHN Three ... foor ... five thirty ...six ten, och six poun' for easy countin' ... ye'll be hopin' 'es widder bides dry for i morn?

GRACE Aye, its been nae bad i day, at least its dry 'ats i main thing. (GRACE RETURNS WITH HER PURSE OPEN)

JOHN Weel 'es is it, ye'll get a puckle fowlk i morn if it's dry.

GRACE Now John, six poun' did ye say. (HANDS OVER THE RIGHT AMOUNT)

JOHN Aye, 'ats it, perfec', thank you wifee.

GRACE Ye'll hae time for a fly?

JOHN Naa, a better nae hinner ye.

GRACE Naa, yer nae hinner 'ins ... awit I'm jist awa ti hae een

misel' so ye better jist sit doon.

JOHN Weel, weel, if yer sure its nae bother.

GRACE Naa, i kettle's biel't onywi' ... tak' a seat. (JOHN SITS AT THE TABLE)

JOHN Yiv a fair puckle stuff here.

GRACE Hud yer tongue, 'ats only i half o it, ye shoold see fit's ben i hoose. (GRACE PROCEEDS TO MAKE THE TEA)

JOHN O aye, it fair mounts up ... it's amazin' i 'mount a shite ye claak ower i 'ears.

GRACE It widni be se bad if it wis jist were ain stuff, bit I forgot 'irs a heep a boxes it belang ti Jess. She left it ahin, ken. God knows if she'll be roupin' 'im or nae ... ye ken fit like aul' foulk are ... niver throw onythin' oot.

JOHN Oh aye, I hoard athin' awa' til I fin' an ess for't ... Aye in fin I div fin an ess for't, I kin niver fin fit I'm lookin' for.

GRACE Ken ess it's a dam' fac'.

JOHN O I ken fit like, futher wis like 'at ... he ess ti hae jam jars 'n tinny's ful' o aul' washers in nuts in bolts, 'n he coold niver fin een i richt size fin ee wis neen een.

GRACE Well God knows fit Jess is gan ti dee wee a ess stuff, anni' dinna ken if she even mins aboot it.

JOHN Ye niver ken she micht hae a feuw antiques murlin' aboot in i bottom o a box.

GRACE O I widni say't, nae n'less a pair a wally dogs ir fleein' dukes are antiques.

JOHN Oh, ye niver ken, I've seen some gie queer lookin' antiques on 'at antiques roadshow, ye coold be sittin' on a goldmine.

GRACE Naa, 'irs only one antique in ess hoose an' 'ats me.

JOHN Och awa we ye, yiv a lang wi ti go 'til yer an antique.

GRACE It's a winner, i 'mount a times I've climb't 'at stair ess weik I feel as bow legg't as a Queen Anne cheer.

(JOHN TAKES A DRINK WHILE CHUCKLING AT GRACE'S REMARK. HE ALSO CASUALLY LOOKS AROUND THE ROOM. HE SEES A PICTURE LEANING AGAINST A WALL THAT TAKES HIS ATTENTION)

JOHN (LEANING FORWARD) God Almighty!! I hinna see een a 'em since I wis knee high ti a chunty.

GRACE Fits 'at? (PEERING TO SEE WHAT JOHN IS LOOKING AT)

JOHN Yer pictire.

GRACE Fit 'at enn, i shires in harness?

JOHN Aye. (STANDS UP AND WALKS TO THE PICTURE) God I min fine fin it eesti hing abeen i fireplace here.

GRACE Div ye min on 'at?

JOHN Oh aye.

GRACE Ye hinna been on i van 'at lang? Hiv ye?

JOHN (RETURNS TO HIS SEAT) Naa, oh naa, 'ats fin futher hid it, fin I wis jist i loon.

GRACE I thocht ye coold niv been 'at aul'.

JOHN Naa ... I div min' ere wis 'is aflest day a sna', jist blin' smore, in I hid ti ging wee futher incase he got stuck. Well we start't comin' up i road in aboot fin we got ti i first corner ken ... ken far it iwis bla's.

GRACE Oh aye, aye.

JOHN Well futher tell't mi ti rin ti i hoose ti get Aul' Dod ti come doon in haul 'im oot wee i tractir, weel fin ay were dein' 'at I wis pit ti i hoose fir a heat at i fire. Weel ye ken fit like Jess is. I wis teen in, tell't ti sit at i bink o i fire 'ere an' geen' a glaas a milk an' a haet scone wee syrip rinin' aff it. It wis i best scone I iver hid, in I min it 'at pictire wee i horse wis hingin' abeen in i fireplace.

GRACE Aye, 'at pictire's been in i go a philly.

JOHN Aye, tis been a gweed feuw 'ear since Aul' Dod deit.

GRACE Aye ... twinty siven 'ear past A'gust.

JOHN You in Dod wereni' lang marry't were ye?

GRACE No, we'd only been marry't in i April o i same 'ear ... I'd hardly gotten ti ken 'em.

JOHN Aye, he wis a topper o a man ... work't 'imsel inti i grun' ... i fairm hid teen i best oot o 'im

... Jess's laist't weel ower i 'ears ...

GRACE Aye, she's deen weel after fit she's wint throu'.. I jist hope i roup i morn's nae ower sair on 'er. Ye'll ask 'er if she's a'richt, bit ye ken fit like, she'd niver say if she wis ir nae.

JOHN Aye, you Stewart wemen are a i same, keep ahin' ti yersels.

GRACE Ers nae time ti moan, 'ers ower muckle ti be deen.

JOHN Aye, it'll be a blae day i morn wee yersels bein' i hinmaist eens aff i hull. I min fine fin I hid i hael roon o i hull ti dee in a Fridi' afterneen, fae Joe Mitchell's, ti Wastie's, ower ti Jake's, sein yersels, 'en doon ti Northies. Noo it's jist yersels, bit fir nae muckle langer.

GRACE Div ye nae ging inby in see were neighbir Jeremy?

JOHN Och, he's a waste a time, I'm sure he's a vegetarian.

GRACE Awa' ye go.

JOHN I'm sure o't, ony time he dis buy onythin' it's only a bitty chucken, he niver his mince or a steak.

GRACE Naa, he widni be, min you he's a gie scranny cheil.

JOHN Aye, 'irs mair fat on a butchers pincil.

GRACE Aye, in you wid ken.

John Aye, that I shoold ... Ach bit ye niver ken, someday i'll mibbee flaag abide in fin wee a hoosekeeper ir a bide-in.

GRACE Weel thi' mun be gie feel ti bide wee i like a him.

JOHN Weel a bit a money an a bit a grun' an a fine big hoose can fair treest i wemen in aboot, spec'ly ti i likes o some o yon toon wemen.

GRACE Aye, bit gee 'em a pair a sharny wellies plyterin' throu' their fine big clean hoose an at 'ill far scunner 'em.

JOHN Aye, yer richt 'are wifee ... well ti hell tho' I'd better awa'. (LOOKS AT THE CLOCK)

GRACE Aye, I better get on misel' less it'll seen be supper-time. (GRACE AND JOHN STAND UP AND MOVE TOWARDS THE DOOR)

GRACE Aye, at lads 'll be in expec'in mate on i table in me nae reidy.

JOHN Aye, 'ats i wye it goes.

GRACE Ats a budy seems ti de ess days is mak' mate ... ye've nae seener made i denner, fin yiv ti think aboot makin' supper, in abeen 'at ye've ti fin time ti dee some bakin' ... It niver stops.

JOHN True enough ... weel ye ken fit i say, it's i belly it keeps i back up.

GRACE I s'pose yer richt 'are. (JOHN OPENS THE DOOR)

JOHN Weel thou' nae dou't I'll see ye i morn.

GRACE Ye comin' up ti i roup are ye?

JOHN Aye, I thocht I'd hae a lookee up by, ken.

GRACE Jist you dee 'at, I'm sure Dod'll be please't ti see ye spec'lly if yer buyin' somethin'.

JOHN Oh, I dinna think I've muckle need for a muck spreader.

GRACE Weel mibbee no.

JOHN Ye kin tell 'im I'll buy 'im a nip, 'at I'll cheer 'im up.

GRACE Oh I dare say it will.

JOHN Weel thou', we'll see ye i morn.

GRACE Aye, weel see ye i morn John, cheerio I've noo ... Aye, cheerio. (GRACE RETURNS TO THE KITCHEN AND THE SCENE ENDS WITH HER STILL SORTING OUT BOXES)

GLOSSARY

Alflest - Almighty
Bourich - Gathering
Boo't - Bent
Clartit - Covered
Dunt - Bang, Knock
Dwam - Daydream, Unconcious
Feart - Frightened
Feet - Place where apprenticeship
          was served
Fathim - Work out
Ferfochan - Tired out
Fooshtie - Old, Rotten
Fyle - While
Flaig - Shock, Scare
Gallivantin' - Roaming around
Gaakin' - Looking
Hashed - Harrassed, Busy
Hinmaist - Last
Lairt - Stuck
Neeper - Neighbour
'oo' bags - Wool bags
Phisog - Face
Puggle't - Overwhelmed with heat
Scunner - Cheesed off
Trauchle - Struggle

North East Hill Farm

Tom Bryan

Wind-bevelled trees dovetail
to sludge cloud frontier.
Dust-familiar outbuildings
fade to stony outcrop,
mortgaged only to wind and rain.

Winter barley ebbs, eddies
in deep beige pools.

Peesies stumble sunward
in their clumsy, perfect roll and pitch.
Rusting tractors shelter magpies
in a weed-choked ditch.

Sunset Song, Revisited

Tom Bryan

I swear I saw Meikleboggs, yesterday,
fumbling with his trouser fly,
spitting at the sun.

Mutch was there too,
nose a'dreep,
polishing his shopfront brass.

Long Rob strides high in the parks,
while John Guthrie wrestles with
seed-time devils.

(I nearly collided with Colquhoun's
rusted bike on his vision road.)
While wind-bent trees swayed
to growling cello chords.

And I saw proud Chris Guthrie
at Tesco's today,
pushing a frozen food trolley,
her body strong and ripe.

It is still a rich human silage (and slurry too)
Rain clouds yet darken the howe.
And Gibbon, listen ...
peesies still sing
to the salt-sea wind.

Thank God

Morag Skene

She was dead before the plate hit the floor!" That's fit the doctor said aboot mi Ma. She wis dryin the dishes an' she jist drappit doon deid. "Jist l-like that! O-oot l-like a lite!" Bill could hardly get oot the words fir greetin. Surely No! We hid bin tae Sunday school, me an' Stan, we wir jist this minute back, bit we couldna be tae blame! Deep doon though ah kent, ah kent fine.

Ye see Ma wis a healthy-lookin woman, tall an' big boned an' as strong as an ox. She wis nae 'oil-paintin' ah suppose, aye afa dour-lookin wi' a nose that stuck richt oot fae her face an' hid a fair bump on it. Ah dinna mean she lookit like a witch, she wisna thin enough fir that.

Ah canna mine the colour o' her een, bit she did hae bonny black hair - shame it wis aye scrapit tae the back o' her heid so naebody ivver saw it - an' thon high colourin so she nivver lookit nae weel, even fin she wis! Ah inheritit that fae mi Ma, that an' her bonny black hair. Stan, that's mi brither, he got her nose - thank god!

Bit the thing ye'd notice very first aboot Ma wis her hands. Great stotters o' things they wir, an' hard? Years o' picklin herrin hid turned the skin tough as aul boots an' twice as roch. "Roch as a badger's arse," Stan wid say, bit then he wis a lot younger than me an' orra wi' it. Onywye, if Ma caught ye wi' the back o' her hand she jist aboot took the skin aff yer lug.

Tae be quite honest we couldna believe it wis that same hands that delivered bairns an' laid oot the deid in oor tenement an' a' the ither tenements roon aboot. Me an' Stan thocht it wisna the smack on the bum that set the bairns aff greetin, it wis the shock o' feelin Ma's hands on their soft wee bodies, an' Stan said it wis jist as weel the folk she laid oot were deid onywye cause Ma wi' a bar o' soap in her hand wis a dangerous thing. Still, fin a' wis said an' deen, her services aye seemed tae be in demand, there wis aye a soul cumin intae the world or leavin it.

It wis Ma's soul ah wis worryin aboot noo, an' mine, an' Stan's. Dr Robertson wis bleeterin on aboot a "heart attack" an' "could happen to anyone" bit ah kent better.

It a' startit a whilie back wi' Da. Puir Da, he wis nivver a weel man, aye poorly. Ah can nivver mine on him workin, Ma hid tae keep us a'. Up at the back o' five in the mornin she'd be, an' awa tae a fish hoose in Fittie, the ither side o' Aiberdeen. Onywye, there wis aye time ah heard the wifies roon aboot sayin Da hid bin 'gassed' in the trenches durin the war. They said, puir Mr Mackie, finivver they spoke aboot him an' lowered their voices as though there wis sum big secret aboot him that only they kent. A' ah can say is thon 'gas' must hae bin afa stuff cause by the time Da climbed the three flights o' stairs tae oor tenement door he wis gaspin for breath that much ye wintit tae breathe for him. It got that bad he nivver steppit ootside the door fae aye wik's end tae the next an' it didna maitter far ye wis in the hoose ye could hear him "breathin". Ma used tae get afa annoyed fin the batteries in the radio wis low cause Da's breathin wid droon it oot a' thegither. That nichts she wid pit him tae his bed afore her favourite 'Book at Bedtime' startit - wi Da protestin a' the wye. "Bit ah'm nae tired woman!" "Yer gaun an' that's that!" she'd say.

At nicht me an' Stan could hear him through the wa bit it wis like the tickin o' a clock, there bit nae there, if ye ken fit ah mean. That's how we aye noticed the nichts it changed. We'd hear his breath cum in great heavin gasps an' the bed wid creak an' groan a' ower the place. Aifter a wee whilie we'd hear Da, wheezin like onythin, say things like, "Ah'm nae fit, ah canna ging on!" or "Fir onysake woman, leave me be!" Then a'thing wid ging deid quiet. That's fin Stan wid creep closer tae me in the bed an' whisper, "Ah wish Da wid finish fitivver they startit Flora cause Ma's gaun tae be in an afa mood in the mornin." An' sure enough the next day if we jist lookit at Ma the wrang wye she wid clap oor lugs. Puir Stan aye got it cause he wis slower than me. Ah aye kept oot o' her wye - thank god!

Sumtimes, the next mornin, her an' Da wid sit glowerin at each ither ower the kitchie table. Aye time ah mine them ha'en an afa row fin Ma said she didna ken how he ivver managed tae get up enough '"wind" tae faither twa bairns! Noo ah kent neeps gave ye wind bit fit neeps an' bairns hid tae dae wi' each ither ah wisna afa sure.

It wis roon aboot the time o' that "afa row" a new meenister came intae oor parish, a Mr Dawson. A nippit-lookin wee mannie he wis wi' beady een an' a gnaffy voice. He'd heard all aboot Mrs Mackie and her services tae the community bit what was this he'd bin hearing, herself bringing souls intae the world and seeing souls oot yet herself and her bairns nivver being seen in church. This jist wisnae guid enough!

Fae ahin the kitchie door me an' Stan could hear Ma unswer in a voice that could clip cloots. "Is that richt?" she said. "Weel, ah hinna hid complaints fae ony o' mi customers yet an' that's mair than ah can say aboot your anes!" Me an' Stan held oor breath bit a' Mr Lawson did wis clear his throat an' say tae Ma, "But what aboot sin, Mrs Mackie. Do you ivver think of sin? We are all sinners in the eyes of the Lord but more so a non-believer like yerself." "Sin! Sin!" Ma roared. "Ye must be jokin man! Ah'm nae even gettin the only sin ah'm allowed tae hae an' you'll ken fit ah mean meenister, you bein a mairrit man ..." It wis like somethin inside Ma hid burst, she jist wint on an' on. It reminded me o' the times ah wid wait fir Ma tae cum hame so ah could clype on Stan an' it wid a' burst oot o' me as se'en as she got in the door. The next meenit we heard Mr Dawson's cup bein banged doon an' he wis aff oot the door as though the divil himsel wis chasin him.

Fit a temper Ma wis in fin he wint awa, she took Stan roon the lug fir nae reason at a' an' jist missed me - thank god! Me an' Stan wir feart tae look her wye.

It must hae bin aboot three wiks aifter the meenister's visit there wis anither afa row got up atween Ma an' Da. Me an' Stan wir jist drappin aff tae sleep fin the creakin an' groanin startit again. Weel a' o' a sudden Da wis shoutin at the tap o' his voice - nae easy wi' his lungs - "Are ye tryin tae kill me woman cause that's fit you an' yer pesterin's daein tae me! Fir the last time, leave me alane!" An' dae ye ken, that wis the last time, the next day Da wis deid!

Ye canna imagine hoo me an' Stan felt fin Mrs Mutch, oor neebour, took us oot ower the bed an' telt us. We stared at each ither an' ah think Stan lookit as feart as ah felt. She'd deen it! She'd pestered him tae death! We kept oor heids doon an' peekit ower at Ma bit there she wis, surrounded by wifies fae oor tenement, greetin her een oot. She didna look much like a murderer bit then ah didna ken fit a murderer wis supposed tae look like. A' this wis too much fir Stan, he burst inta tears an' wint runnin ower tae Ma bit she jist pushed him awa an' telt him he wis the man o' the hoose noo an' couldna be seen greetin like a bairn. That fair stoppit Stan in his tracks an' a look o' sheer terror crossed his face. "Bit ah'll still be sleepin in the same bed as Flora win't ah Ma, ah will win't ah?" Oor neebours an' Ma lookit at him as though he'd gone wrang in the heid.

The hoose wis afa quiet wi' Da's breathin bein awa. Safe tae say we missed that mair than we missed Da himsel. Fir us, me an' Stan, naethin much hid changed. Ma still wint tae work packin herrin ivvery mornin - wearin her 'blacks' o' course - folk cairrit on ha'en bairns an' deein an' me an' Stan wint tae school an' did oor chores. Fir some reason though Ma wisna sae coorse-tempered ony mair, nae sae ready tae lift her hand. We thocht she wis cumin doon wi' somethin.

It must hae bin the same time ah won the Bursary for Aiberdeen Central School - aboot a year aifter Da dee'd - fin Ma flummoxed us wi' her bit o' news. "Ah'm gettin mairrit again bairns!" she said. Me an' Stan jist lookit at her wi' open moos. Far hid she found this mannie an' did he ken fit she'd deen tae the last ane? Sumbody should warn him! Onywye, up he cum that same nicht tae meet us. He wis a tall, an' ah suppose, for mi Ma, a good-lookin man bit me an' Stan were jist stammergastit - he wis the local scaffie! He sweepit the streets roon aboot oor tenements, we kent him fine! Me an' Stan wir jist black affrontit! Tae mak things worse we hid tae pass him ivvery day on oor wye tae school. Weel, ye've nae idea the performance wi hid aifter that nicht tryin tae avoid him an' fin he did see us he wid shout oot, "Aye,aye bairns, tell yer Ma ah'll be up the nicht tae see her!" O' course if we'd pals wi' us we'd try an' nae let on he wis spikin tae us. Bit there wis tae be nae escape cause on the tenth o' June, nineteen hunred an' thirty Ma mairrit Bill an' fae then on wis kent as Mrs McDonald, the "scaffie's wife" an' we were kent as Flora an' Stan, the "scaffie's bairns".

Strange that it wis aboot this time that Ma found 'religion'. Weel, fit ah mean is, she found it fir me an' Stan cause they wir nae seener mairrit fin we wir shooed oot the door tae Sunday School. This wis so her an' Bill could hae a lang lie like maist ither folk did on a Sunday. The funny thing wis, she nivver seemed tae need ane fin Da wis alive. Onywye, even Mr Dawson noticed oor regular attendance an' mentioned it tae Ma . "This," he said, "must be due tae the "influence" o' your new husband, Mrs McDonald." "Indeed!" said Ma, "Mr McDonald's influence is makin an afa difference tae mi life!" There must hae bin somethin in Ma's unswer Mr Dawson didna like, cause he narrawed his beady een an' peered afa suspiciously at Ma - fa jist stared richt back at him. Mr Dawson's courage failed him real quick an' he nipped awa mutterin somethin aboot hopin tae see them baith in church. "Huh! Ah've found better things tae dae wi' mi time on a Sunday!" Ma shoutit aifter him. Ah fair thocht we were a' gaun tae burn in hell - noo that ah kent aboot sic a place - Ma spikin tae a man o' God like that.

Ah wis wrang, though, cause naethin terrible happened tae us an' life wint on. Ah startit at the Central in the A'gust an' Stan bawled his heid aff cause we couldna ging tae school thegither ony mair. Ah telt him tae stop greetin like a jessie or a'body wid laugh at him. Bill, oor step-da, wis guid tae us - thank god - an', in time, we even got ower the shame o' him bein a scaffie. Ma wis a different wifie a' thegither an' even wint aboot wi' a smile on her face sumtimes.

Mind you, that wis seen wipit aff the day a neebour, a nosy besom, telt Ma that Maisie Buchan hid bin heard invitin Bill in, "Fir yer fly-cup Mr McDonald, ony time ye'r passin." Noo this Maisie hid a kirn o' bairns bit naebody ivver ca'ed her Mrs Buchan, it wis aye, "That Maisie Buchan!". Ah wis fair fascinatit wi' Maisie. She aye hid on bricht reed lipstick - through the day! Onywye, oot wint Ma tae the backie, stood there wi' her shovels o' hands on her hips an' bawled oot, "Maisie Buchan, ye man-stealin bitch, cum oot here this minute, ah wint tae spik tae ye!" Afore ye kent it, heids appeared fae a'wye. This wis the maist excitement they'd hid since Mrs Finnies false teeth fell oot o' her moo fin she wis leanin oot ower her tenement winda spikin tae Mrs Mutch, fa swore she wid hae bin markit fir life if she hidna dived oot o' the road sae quick. Stan couldna see fit a' the fuss wis aboot cause he thocht Mrs Mutch hid a face like the back end o' a bus onywye.

Oot came Maisie, knee-deep in bairns, lipstick flashin (she didna disappoint me) airms crossed, stockins rolled doon tae her unkles, an' she didna even look feart! Fit wis a' this shoutin aboot, she wis askin. Ma winted tae ken fit wis she playin at, invitin her Bill inta that "tip" she hid the brass neck tae ca' a hoose? Maisie said Ma hid naethin tae worry aboot, she didna funcy men wi' "afflictions" onywye. That made Ma tak a second notion tae hersel. "Fit dae ye mean 'afflictions', there's naethin wrang wi' mi man!" Ma shoutit. "Yer jokin," said Maisie, "his eye-sicht must be bad afore he mairrit an ugly cow like you!" Noo ah did think that wis an afa coorse thing tae say. Ma wisna ugly, she jist wisna bonny. Weel, that wis it! A' hell broke loose! They were shoutin an' sweerin at each ither wi' the neebours, hopin for a guid fecht, eggin them on fin a' o' a sudden Ma stuck ane o' her muckle fists richt under Maisie's nose an' telt her if she ivver caught her messin aboot wi' her man she'd knock her heid through the nearest wa'. Aye look at that hand helpit Maisie decide she wisna interestit in scaffies onywye, she could dae much better for hersel. That wis guid enough for Ma an' wi' a look o' triumph she grabbed a haud o' me an' Stan an' shoved us afore her through the crowd o' wifies. Me an' Stan felt 'fair airchie' ha'en a Ma that a'body wis feart o', so we couldna get ower the brass neck o' Maisie fin she shoutit oot - fae a safe distance - "At least he widna hae tae pit a paper bag ower my heid fin he bedded me!" Ma nivver turned a hair, she kent she'd won.

A' the excitement must hae gone tae Ma's heid cause that very nicht she startit pesterin Bill. We could hear a' the aul familiar noises only this time there wis nae angry voice. Me an' Stan were terrified. "Fit if she kills this ane Flora? Ah like Bill, ah dinna wint him tae dee, onywye the next ane micht nae be sae fine." So the twa o' us made 'the deal', then pit oor heids under the blunkets an' hummed tae oorsels so we couldna hear ony mair.

An' this is fit's cum o' it. Ma starin an' starin at the kitchie reef wi' her moo hingin open an' Bill kneelin next tae her wi' his heid in his hands, rockin an' moanin. Of course he disna ken me an' Stan saved his life, ye see, we made a deal wi' God the ither nicht - if he saved Bill we'd ging tae Sunday School for the rest o' oor days, an' that's a lang, lang time.

Standin here though ah'm thinkin maybe it's got naethin tae dae wi' God, maybe me an' Stan hiv inherited her terrible power jist like ah've got her colour an' her hair an' Stan's got her nose ... "Fit's wrang wi' Ma Flora, why's she nae gettin up? Why's Bill greetin like that?"

Aye, he's aye bin slow his Stan - thank god!

War Memorial: Inverurie
S B Campbell

From my window I see him
Every day, standing in the market square,
Braced at attention, silent and as still
As the statue he is.
Rain pours down on him, as it would
On Flanders or Ypres.
Black crows sit on shoulders, arms and head
As they would on Flanders or Ypres.
Will your staring features answer me?
What woman from hell, Chieftain's descedant
Or farm loon
Are you modelled on?
That solid chest, those hard muscles.
From whose dragging clay furrows
Were your raw elements sucked?
The man
On Flanders or Ypres.
Brave Caledonia;
Your young men and ploughmen
Lie well drilled; dying for others.
No sunrise will spring them
Verdant again.

Davy
S B Campbell

The trees are at the penultimate stage;
A splendour of rich gold and warm bronze.
Yes, I know
You've always had coppers in your pocket,
But it is a good time, for you Davy,
To write the last chapter, so you tell me.
This is the pay off;
Your hand shake is more than golden to me.

The Tay is cold, but see how yet
A patch of silver sun (yes, cold steel)
But how it cuts and dazzles
Through Autumn's dimming of the mists.

Not many miles now, it hasn't taken long.
From the old house, turned silent,
Boarded up with your wife's memory.
No children open it with laughter.

Not many miles from evergreen country
To the city changes....

Davy is dizzy on his feet sometimes,
Was a Shop Steward sometime,
Wants to go home,
Anytime.

Icebound
Greg Dawson Allen

What happens when the crew of a 19th century Scottish whaling ship bound northwards to the Arctic sea in search of depleting numbers of whales find themselves at the mercy of the elements and... icebound?

On board the crew desperately fight to keep the stricken ship clear of the crushing ice floes. Among them are three men of different generations who are reminded of their fragile mortality and forced by their circum-stances to confront emotional and unresolved issues of their past.

Woven into their conflict is the colourful ship's figurehead - once a magnificent oak tree torn from the forest to become the carved and painted reluctant symbol of luck and good fortune to the superstitious seafarers - a light shining in the cramped, dark world of the whalers and the protagonist in each of the men's unfolding inner conflicts.

FIGUREHEAD:
Through darkness lit by the moon
the branches animated the eye of the artist
who watched in fascination
the patterns caper over the lichen canvas
antics taking on form
creating illusions
for idolatress adventure
on the journey towards each destiny
passing on visions to mute onlookers
more than they could keep to themselves
and so
many voices were given to the protagonists
of cryptic reality

Before the storyteller spoke
the Oakmen sat in judgement
gloating over the trespassers
eating from the poisoned plate
those who dared to tread beneath
the groined arches above
a material blanket
where once upon a life
we were conceived

Long before the forests were called ancient
the trees were safe in the care of the Oakmen
once keepers of a terrestrial realm

have now fled their earthen homes

Then the Druids came and set the stones
as temples to the spirits
offering gifts to the dormant labyrinths
whilst the Oakmen became characters
in the storyteller's yarns

The Priests knew no more no less
than demanding loyalty and purity
from the dependants
at a stroke
of a circumcision blade

Our acorns danced to Jupiter
and woven leafy limbs gave shelter
to the catalysts of a new age

I felt my body split
by tools of stone and metal
the wedge of needless torture
driven deep into the heart

Fingers of torn wood point upwards
in defiance of the sacrilege
to a leafless body
ringed with life

bitten by the smiling teeth
of the sharpened saw
spitting oil into the wounds
in silent insult

Their aproned surgeons wanking
with mallet and chisel
across torn wood
as sharp as the tongues of men
stripping away the layers
searching for my heart

A thousand pieces fell to the floor
as each cut sculpted
a tortured shape of lust
inspired by feeble faith
into the image of the concubine

At her feet are laid the riches
the spoils of war
triumphant trophies from the frozen battlefield

I may face towards your destination
and not see the way ahead
nor do I care
do not expect me to be a shield against
dilemmas of your own doing

A light in the darkness of greed

Response to 'Icebound'
A G Day

Three men stand in a darkened room
steel hulls hollowed tomb
raging storms a winter's squall
to the sound of the seagulls' silent call
cracking ice on a wooden beam
sunless sky
a whaler's scream
'There she blows!'
and dives again
whalers thrown spike divides
one part wood - the other pain
and floats to a sea of shame
windswept craggen faced
a whaler's scar
mapped before as kills
the ocean rolls with ice like moves
three men stand in a darkened room.

Older one to younger;
'Oak or ash our Figurehead?'
sweet prudence
'Neptune's dread
he'll not call while she's aboard
nor her to him will see.'
Thunderous crack on the starboard aft
ropes bound tight the whaler's lash
middle one of three with hook in hand
to the blowing whale now sinks his shaft
another scream and yet still more
the clouds part and the sun is seen
'Sweet prudence, was it you I heard sing
or the flaying knife to the pilot's skin?'
Barrels roll on tempered steel
with oil drenched flesh to the killers kiln
but now no more whales for the whaler's
dream.

Jimmy 'Scout' MacBeath

Stan Gerry

Scout threw off his plaid and sat up leaning against the castle wall as he rubbed the sleep from his eyes. It wasn't the first time he had spent a night in the ruins of the Boyne Castle. He had left Banff the previous night in some haste. In fact, he always seemed to leave Banff in a bit of a hurry. Scout smiled to himself. He knew he could always get the Banffers going when he broke into 'McPherson's Rant'.

"Get oot o' here ye damned tink," the bobby had snapped at him as he sat on the steps of the Plainstones. Scout rose hastily to his feet and glanced at the bobby, a mischevious smile on his face.

"It wisnae me that hung McPherson," he announced as he strode off then stopped in mid-stride, looked up at the clock tower and raising his arm pointed upwards. "An' yer k-nock's still five meenits faist," he accused.

The bobby rose to the insult like a trout to a fly as the barbed remark struck home. "MacBeath ye've got twa meenits tae get oot o' the toon," he threatened.

"I'm awa, I'm awa," retorted Scout hastily. "In twa meenits ye winna see me for stew an' sma' steens," and, with an exaggerated salute, he took to his heels.

Gathering a few twigs and branches from around where he had slept he quickly built a small fire and, taking a soot blackened syrup can from his ex-army small pack, he strode down to the Boyne burn and dipped the can in the burn to fill it. Returning to the fire to set the can amidst the flames, he squatted down and waited for it to come to the boil. Delving into his small pack again, he found his crumpled almost empty quarter pound pack of Lyons tea and shook some into the now boiling water. Setting the can to one side, he rummaged in his pack for the tin of condensed milk he had bought in Banff, pierced the top of the can with his pocket knife and dribbled the syrupy liquid into the steaming can of tea. Humming the tune of 'The Bonnie Lass O' Fyvie O', he took a sip from the steaming can. "Jesus that's hate," he spluttered and set the can at his feet to cool. His thoughts drifted to his previous visit to Portsoy and his run in with Jock Rennie the bobby.

He had walked from Huntly to Cornhill and intended spending the night there, but the offer of half a crown to help a drover deliver a flock of one hundred sheep to Kindrought farm on the outskirts of Portsoy was too good a chance to miss, especially as he had been given the money before setting out. All he had to do was stand at the end of the farm tracks and stop the sheep from wandering off the road. The drover's dog did most of the work and Scout's half crown was easily earned. Declining the offer of a bed for the night in the farm chaumber, Scout set out for Portsoy, his half crown destined for the till in the Shore Inn. There were worse places to spend the evening and if 'Fat Tommy Jars' and 'Alickie Farties' were there so much the better. Besides, Mrs Duncan the landlady enjoyed listening to his corn kisters and bothy ballads. That was worth at least one free dram.

Fat Tommy and Alickie Farties, along with an assortment of others, were already in the bar when Scout made his entrance. "Fit like Scout?" was Fat Tommy's bellowed welcome.

"Nae sae bad, nae sae bad Tom," asserted Scout.

"I hear ye wiss chased oot o' Banff again Scout. Fa gave ye the heave iss time?" queried Alicky.

"Och een o' the bobbies," confessed Scout.

"Wiss his name McPherson by ony chance?" laughed Fat Tommy.

"It micht hae been," surmised Scout a smile on his lips. "I nivver stoppit tae ask".

"Ah weel hae a dram an' sit doon an' gi'e us yer news," offered Fat Tommy. Scout nodded his head eagerly and watched intently as Mrs Duncan poured the whisky into a copper measure then tipped it into a glass.

"Lang may yer lum reak wi' ither fowk's coal," toasted Scout and drained his glass.

As the night wore on, Scout's corn kisters and bothy ballads had feet tapping, the requests coming one after the other, his only respite coming when he could plead, "I'll hae tae wet my fussle."

"I dinna ken fit wye ye can mind them a' Scout," said Mrs Duncan as she
called last orders.

"It's a gift. It's a gift," declared Fat Tommy belching loudly.

"Ye must hae ben born wi' it," interpolated Alicky Farties.

"Aye nae doobt," agreed Scout, fingering the unspent half crown in his
pocket.

As Mrs Duncan shepherded them out of the door, Fat Tommy turned to
Scout. "I canna ask ye roon bye Scout, Maggie Elsie'll hae the door lockit
or noo. She's nae affa keen on lettin' me in fan I've hae'n a dram."

"Ach that's often the wye o't Tom," observed Scout. "Ah weel I'll jeest
kip doon in the salmon bothy," decided Fat Tommy with a tired sigh. Scout
was glad Tommy did not offer him the dubious comforts of the salmon
bothy. He had spent one night in the bothy with him some six months ago
and had told everyone in the Shore Inn the following evening that, "It wiss
like tryin' tae sleep in a thunner storm athoot the lichtnin'." The rumbles
emitting from Tommys ample torso had kept him awake most of the night.

"Aye I'll awa an' get my heid doon somewye an' a' Tom," said Scout and
headed off into the darkness up the steep incline of Church Street. Scout
paused at the top of Church Street. Jim Geddes a long-time acquaintance
lived at number one and there was shed at the back of the house which he
knew was never locked. For a brief moment, he toyed with the idea of spending the night there but thought better of it. Jim's wife, Elsie, had as Scout
put it, "A tongue that could clip cloots". If she found him in the shed in the
morning, he might not survive the tongue lashing. With a wry smile and a
shrug of his shoulders he turned into Seafield Street and headed for the
railway station. He knew there would be goods' wagons in the sidings or
maybe, with a bit of luck, he might even manage to spend the night in the
waiting room.

Finding the station waiting room closed, Scout's only option was one of
the goods' wagons in the sidings and he was fortunate to find one empty. He
slid the door open. As he clambered inside it, he realised why the door had
been left open. "Gyad the pong," muttered Scout. The wagon had recently

been used to transport fish and had been left open to dry out. Scout slept well despite the fishy aroma. He was wakened abruptly to the sound of Jock Rennie's voice. "Come on, oot o' there Scout," he ordered not unkindly. "Ye've nae business in there."

Scout shrugged off his plaid and, grasping his pack, lowered himself to the ground. "Nae hairm meant Jock," stated Scout.

"I ken that Scout," affirmed Jock with a smile. "Ye micht hae pickit a better een than that though," he added, his nostrils assailed by the smell of fish which clung to Scout's clothes.

"Ony port in a storm Jock," replied Scout, giving his plaid a vigorous shake and tossing it over his shoulder. He looked earnestly at Jock.

"Aye awa wi' ye Scout," ordered Jock. "Mak yer feet yer best freen."

Scout nodded his gratitude. "At least ye didna ca' me a tink Jock."

"Och the Banffers hiv a persecution complex Scout," said Jock smothering a smile.

"Is that fit wye their k-nock's five meenits fast?" asked Scout.

"Could be, Scout," answered Jock, "but dinna ask them."

The Travels of Jimmy 'Scout' MacBeath
Stan Gerry

Jock Rennie watched Scout stride out of the station yard and smiled to himself at the thought of Scout taunting the Banff bobby with the hanging of the outlaw Macpherson. Jock knew that Scout could never resist the temptation to remind the Banffers of the historical piece of folklore that made some of the town's inhabitants cringe with embarrassment.

As he turned into Seafield street Scout had a quick glance at the town clock noting that it was not yet seven o'clock. He silently cursed Jock Rennie for his almost pre-dawn reveille and smiled ruefully as he recalled Jock's expression when his nostrils caught the unique stale fish bree aroma clinging to Scout's clothing. Scout felt desperately in need of a cup of tea. Suddenly inspired by the thought he fingered the as yet unspent half crown in his trews pocket and quickening his pace hastened for Donald the bakers farther along Seafield Street. For the price of a half dozen fresh butteries he felt sure he could pay Jim Geddes and his wife a call. The offer of the butteries would be sure to take the edge off Elsie's caustic remarks his unexpected visit was sure to elicit.

"God that smell's gan roon my hert like a hairy worm," enthused Scout, the fragrance of new baked bread drifting round his head as he entered the shop. Pocketing the change from his half crown and clutching the still warm butteries in a bag he set off back along Seafield Street for the home of Jim Geddes and his wife. Almost drooling at the thought of a hot cup of sweet tea and a buttery to go with it Scout had to resist the almost overpowering temptation to stuff one of the butteries in his mouth and eat it on the spot. Elsie Geddes was on her knees scrubbing the steps of number one Church Street vigorously when Scout appeared.

"Fit like Elsie?" enquired Scout.

She paused and looked up at him. "Nae ony the better o' you speirin'," she snapped at him and resumed scrubbing with increased vigour.

It was far too early in the morning for Elsie to be civil to anyone and

Scout was not in the least bit offended by the rebuff. Rising to her feet Elsie sloshed the remaining water in her bucket across the steps and Scout had to skip aside to avoid having his tartan trews drenched.

"Ye're an affa quine Elsie," he declared, a smile on his lips.

"Jim's nae in Scout," she announced "He's awa checkin' his snares." Scout heaved a sigh of despair. There would be no cup of tea unless Jim was in residence. Taking the bag of butter rolls from the folds of his plaid, he handed them to Elsie.

"Far's he got them set Elsie?" he enquired as she accepted the gift.

"Half wye up the C'hythe brae" she informed him. "He's nae lang awa," she added. Scout knew that the unsolicited gift of half a dozen butter rolls was the only reason for Elsie divulging where her husband was and what he was doing.

"I'll awa up the brae an' see if he's ta'en a rabbit Elsie," decided Scout. He knew that Jim only ever set two or three snares and seldom failed to take a rabbit wherever he set them. He was countryman born and bred and wartime rationing was no particular hardship to Jim or Scout for that matter. Living off whatever nature provided would have been their lifestyle, war time or not. Scout crossed the little bridge spanning the Durn burn and hiked up the steel incline of the Cowhythe brae. He spotted Jim stopping to take a rabbit from a snare and called out.

"Ye got a denner 'an Jim."

"Aye Scout," asserted Jim. "This een winna nibble nae mair neeps."

Scout fell into step beside Jim as they headed back downhill. "Elsie said that ye wis oot at yer wires Jim," declared Scout explaining his finding Jim.

"Fit did ye dae Scout, cross her palm wi' silver?" queried Jim.

"Na, na, jeest a half a dozen o' George Donald's butteries," answered Scout with a laugh.

"Weel weel, wi' your butteries an' this rabbit we micht be in her gweed books Scout," said Jim hopefully.

"D'ye still fish the burn Jim?" enquired Scout as they crossed the little bridge at the foot of the Cowhythe brae.

"Michty aye Scout," confirmed Jim. "There's aye a troot tae be ta'en noo an' again," he added. The little burn was another source of food for Jim.

His skill with his little green heart trout fly rod was often put to good use during the summer months and the thought of brown trout rolled in oat meal and fried in butter made Jim wish the fishing season was started instead of still being more than a month away.

"Och, I hinna the patience for fishing wi' a rod Jim," stated Scout. "Mind ye I've guddled mair than my fair share I suppose," he confessed.

Jim gave Scout a disapproving look. "Well I suppose ther's a knack tae that," he conceded.

"Aye ye've tae ken fitna boulder they're under," agreed Scout. "Nae doobt ye hiv tae ken far tae set a wire for a rabbit," he added in a conciliatory tone. Scout knew that Jim always sought permission before setting snares and the grieve at Cowhythe was sure to find the odd rabbit or hare hanging form his door knob now and again. Jim was no poacher and never abused the privilege of being allowed to take a rabbit or hare for his own use.

"Elsie should hae the kettle on the bile or noo Scout," surmised Jim as they approached his home. Jim's remark was as good as an invitation to Scout.

"A drappie tay wid be grand Jim I'm spittin' feathers," he declared with feeling.

Elsie was pouring boiling water from her cast iron kettle into the teapot as they entered the kitchen. Jim placed the rabbit on the kitchen sink draining board. Taking his few snares from his jacket pocket hung them on a hook behind the kitchen door and sat down at the kitchen table.

"Ye dinna leave yer snares oot a' the time?" observed Scout, taking a seat opposite Jim at the table.

"Na na Scout, I widna ha'e them lang if I did that," replied Jim. "There's mair than me taks a rabbit aff Cowhythe grun' an' nae a' the rabbits come oot o' their ain snares. I jeest set mine at nicht an' lifts them in the mornin'."

Elsie set out three enamel mugs pouring tea into each of them. "Sugars a' deen bit, I've a drappie seerup if ye wint it," offered Elsie.

"Fine deen Elsie quine," enthused Scout, dipping a tea spoon into the can and winding the toffee like syrup on his spoon before stirring it into his tea.

"Oh dammit," cursed Elsie "I forgot a' aboot the butteries," and dashed to the kitchen range where she had placed them in the little oven to keep warm. "That's your wyte Scout," she exclaimed, casting Scout an accusing glance as she dropped the piping hot butteries on the table.

"I didna mind a thing aboot them Elsie," lied Scout. He knew perfectly well that Elsie would have been affronted had he reminded her of his gift. "Nae hairm deen Elsie," said Scout sinking his teeth into a crisp buttery. "Man a body could get eesed tae this Jim," declared Scout scooping the crumbs from the table and tossing them into his mouth.

Jim smiled as he reached for another buttery. "Aye it mak's a change fae the usual bowl o' brose," agreed Jim.

"Weel, weel the meal winna be wasted," remarked Elsie. "It's skirlie an' tatties for denner."

Scout glanced out of the kitchen window and gave out with an amused laugh. "I see Jimmy Cooper hisnae got brakes on 'is bike yet," he observed.

"Jimmy Cooper's niver hid brakes on 'is bike," stated Jim. "He aye walks doon braes an' pedals up 'em."

"If he didnae ha'e tae come intae the toon for his mither and faither's pension he'd nivver be aff the croft," interpolated Elsie.

Jim had known the Coopers for many years and their croft Greenriggs of Badenspink was often visited by Jim during the summer months, when the Coopers welcomed his help with the hoeing, haymaking and harvest. Cash seldom changed hands for Jim's labours. A few eggs, a farmhouse cheese or even butter would be the Coopers means of payment and Jim was always on hand to keep the rabbits and hares in check. A fat cockerel or two was always delivered during the festive season and it pleased Elsie no end to receive the gift. She loathed plucking with a passion and an oven ready bird was a rare treat at that time. Not many would have seen a fowl of any description grace their table at the start of the nineteen fifties. The almost reclusive lifestyle of many of Banffshire's crofters of that period were to be the last of a dying breed. With their passing would go many of the skills of the pre-merchanised age heralded by the new breed of tractors appearing on the scene, with hydraulics being one of the great benefits of the new age in farming.

"Here Scout, there wis a mannie lookin' for ye here a few weeks ago," announced Elsie suddenly.

"Fa wid that ha'e been 'an Elsie lass?" enquired Scout a puzzled look on his face.

"It was a mannie fae the B.B.C." Elsie informed him. "He said that somebody telt 'im we kent ye an' he wis wunnerin' far he cwid fin' ye."

"The B.B.C. Elsie, fit wid they be needin' wi' the likes o' me?" mused Scout.

"He said that he wid like ye tae sing some o' yer cornkister an' bothy ballads on the wireless," answered Elsie.

"Awa wi' ye Elsie yer ha'en me on," chided Scout.

"Na na it's true Scout," Elsie retorted indignantly.

"Aye it's true Scout," confirmed Jim. "The mannie telt me 'imsel'," he added.

"Wid ye gang an' sing on the wireless Scout?" queried Elsie, her curiosity getting the better of her.

"The mannie said that they wid pey ye Scout," said Jim, a note of envy in his voice.

"Weel that wid mak' a change," replied Scout "I've nivver sung for siller afore."

"Nae in Banff onywye," stated Elsie wickedly. The news of Scout's hasty departure from Banff had obviously reached Elsie's ears and she could not resist the chance to comment on it.

Scout's features broke into a cheeky grin. "If the B.B.C. wint me tae sing on the wireless, I'll gi'e them McPherson's rant for nithin'," he remarked, drumming his fingers on the table.

"Ye better nae sing onything aboot Portsoy," warned Elsie, her voice full of menace.

"I dinna ken ony sangs aboot Portsoy coal bags," jibed Scout, ducking his head in mock fear as Elsie raised her hand in threat.

"I've a gweed mind tae come aff yer lug a dirl," she shrilled.

Jim rose from the table, noting the light of battle in his wife's eyes.

Keen to avoid a confrontation between Elsie and Scout, he strode over to the kitchen sink and taking the rabbit by the hind legs nodded towards the door.

"I'll skin this afore I forget," he said and sighed with relief when Scout took the hint and rose to follow him.

"By God, ye hiv tae keep yer heid doon fan Elsie gets 'er dander up Jim," exclaimed Scout as he watched Jim expertly skin the rabbit in the shed behind the house.

"Weel it's yer ain wyte Scout," retorted Jim unsympathetically. 'Think yersel' lucky she wisnae in a bad mood."

Scout exploded in a burst of laughter at Jim's remark. "Weel weel Jim, a black cra' winna wash fyte," surmised Scout. His remark meaning that Elsie was very unlikely to change character. "I think I'll awa Jim," decided Scout suddenly, the wanderlust upon him again.

"Fit if that mannie fae the B.B.C. comes seekin' ye again Scout?' asked Jim.

Scout paused for a moment, frowned in concentration then replied. "Tell 'im tae speir at Jock Rennie."

"Nae muckle wunner naebody ivver kens far tae find ye Scout, ye nivver bide affa lang in ae place," declared Jim.

Scout laughed heartily. "True enough Jim," conceded Scout. "Nae muckle fowk ivver ken far tae find me but I'm nivver tint."

"Aye, yer richt there Scout, an' I ken mair than ae cra' that winna wash fyte," called Jim as he waved him goodbye.

The Flittin
Kathleen Smith

Sic a fiasco I've nivver seen,
in a' 'e days I've lived an' breathed,
as ma auntie Jemmima's flittin.
They'd a len o a larry fae ma cousin
Ben,
it wid've been better aff left at hame,
we could've carriet a'thing quicker.

Ye heard it rattlin doon 'e street,
lang afore ye even seen't.
It broch oot a' 'e neighbours.
An' ence it wis stoppit, it widnae start,
nae matter fu muckle he priggit an' tried,
till he finally lost his timper.

Well they'd load it up an' try again,
an' at's fan a' 'e fun began,
as 'e hoose began tae empty.
Uncle Geordie wis standin tall,
gein oot orders tae een an' a',
like he wis back in 'e army.

Autie Jemmima wi a bricht reid face
wis fleein aboot a' o'er 'e place,
an' sae wis cousin Sally.
Ma brither Billy got pinned tae 'e wa',
wi a chest o' drawers 'at Ben let fa
on 'e taes o ma cousin Harry.

Harry wis hoppin' aboot wi rage,
an' knocket o'er 'e budgie's cage,
so oot flew little Jocky.
Ma uncle Geordie banged tee 'e
door,
an' knockit peer Sally on tae 'e floor,
as he lunged tae catch 'e birdie.

Bit Jocky wis o'er glad tae be free,
he chirpit awa a sang o' glee,
an' made for 'e open windae.
"Oh no," ma auntie Jemmima cried,
bit alas 'e windae wis open wide,
an' oot flew 'e budgie.

Oot came 'e cage tae sit on 'e dyke,
tae trice 'e cocky little tyke,
bit he wis nae sae feel.
He chirpit oot a happy tune,
an' above 'e cage flew roon an' roon,
an' then he disappeared.

He wis nivver tae be seen again,
an' a' because o' ma cousin Ben,
wi' yon stupid chest.
Bit on 'e flittin hid tae gang,
an' on tae 'e larry 'e cage wis flung,
alangside a' 'e rest.

Well finally it wis loaded up,
a bit lopsided, (I thocht it wid coup)
an' Ben wis ready tae start it.
A' body prayed 'at it wid gang,
an' till 'is day I'll nivver ken,
fit wye he got it roadit.

Bit aff we wint wi't doon 'e road,
creakin' an' swayin' fae side tae side,
we got tae their new address.
An' as a'body startit tae pile oot 'er,
Jemmima stept forrit tae open e door
an' fell o'er an auld kist.

As she wint tumblin' on tae 'e grun,
'e key wint fleein' an' fell doon 'e drain,
an' a we heard wis sploosh!
'e een an' only key wis tint,
an' 'e back door een hidnae been sint,
it wis inside 'e hoose.

So aff came 'e cover o' 'e drain,
an' cowerin o'er wis cousin Ben,
tae see fit he could fin.
Efter poukin an' proddin' wi a stick,
He finally managed tae get it oot,
an' cleaned it up again.

Fit else could possibly gang wrang noo,
I'm sure wis 'e thochts in a'body's
broo,
as Geordie opened 'e door.
We steppit inside an' looked aroon,
a'thing wis bonny, shinnin' an' clean,
bit ootside it hid started tae poor.

We set tae an' shifted 'e load,
as quick as we humanly could,
an' 'e rain began tae clear.
An' jist fin a'thing wis gan' alang fine,
a howl got up fae at cousin o' mine,
as he skinnt his han' on 'e door.

The bleed wis poorin' fae his wound,
an' Lord almichty fit a soun',
we thocht at he wis dein'.
Bit auntie Jemmima shooed him awa,
tae tend tae his peer an battered paw,
while Sally stood tee heein'.

There's only one mair thing I'll say,
I wis glad tae see 'e end o' 'at day.
Let it nivver be repeated.
It'll gang doon in oor faimily history,
an' I wid say 'at there's mair an' me,
will nivver evir forget it.

The Makkin o the Lan
Christine Ritchie

Unkent forces deep doon in th' intimmers o the earth
Tyaaved an ettled sair ti meet heid on in a stramash,
Shoved sidieweys, nae carin fit they shoogled on the wey
An lurkit up the grun in muckle faulds wi a their fash.

Sae cam the ancient range o Monadh liath an Cairngorm,
Soarin' heids weel-happed in clood an claikin wi the sun,
But pickit at by rain an frost an win an winter snaas,
The greatest fun theirsels worn doon near level wi the grun.

Noo ither forces tyaaved deep doon aneth the fashious crust
An massive blocks o worn doon lan wis heaved up fae ablow
A muckle crack split Alba in twa fae coast ti coast
An shouder ti grey shoulder stood the Bens o the plateau.

Syne cam the muckle ice ti haud the lan in cauldreich thrall
O winter, till a warmer world furlt roon ti brak the spell
An runes were scratched on ilky rock as hills were rypit bare
Fan the slitherin ice slid seaward an the lan wis left itsel.

Roon-backit hills like muckle beasties cooried doon ti sleep,
Deep straths delved oot atween them wi the glaciers' doonward flow
Wee chappt-aff valleys clingin, hingin til the mountainside
As burnies loup in waterfaas ti reach the flair below.

Fit a scourin an a scrapin, grun an steens taen hyne awa
Till the sheets o ice, forfochen, grun doon slowly til a halt,
Dumpin aa their coorse moraine, they meltit clean awa
Wi Buchan lan a sottar an the Muckle Glen a fault.

An shairly noo the forces o the earth maun bide at peace
Wi aa the grun throwither an nae fit fur beast or man.
Wi graivel, steen an caul weet clay, bog an dubs an mire
Atween the Deveron an the Don, a dour, teuch, ill-faured lan.

Bit syne the fyowk, wi swite-weet hoors o darg wi pick an ploo
Drain't the watter, gaither't steens, mixed clorty clay wi san
Vrocht parks, bricht gowd wi ripplin corn, green wi win-tickled girse
Far, siccart in wi drysteen waas, nowt graze on gweed ferm lan.

Iss Hoose
Christine Ritchie

Iss hoose
Far I wis born
Ma faither sint awa
Ti wanner
Aa the file
The weemen gaed aboot
Their weemen's work
Hame in i hinner eyne
Ti fin a bairn
An warmth ootside
An in himsel

Iss hoose
Files fit ti burst
Wi bairns, at cam
Fae baith sides o
The family
Runnin ower i road
Wi tarry feet,
Paddlin in soughin watters

O a freenly firth
An killin clean
Steen deid
Ony thocht
An anely bairn
Wis lanesome

Iss hoose
Faa's door stood open aye
Ti welcome in
The bricht licht o
The simmer sun,
Stored anent
The cauldreich days
o winter
Far, sat in snaw dim kitchen
Neth i skylicht
Roon i glowin range
We toastit
Steamin socks

Iss hoose
Far ma puir mither
Wannert
Lost
Far she hid been
The keystane,
Baker o bonnie bannocks,
Shewer o fine claes,
Stringth o the nae weel
In body an in hert,
Her coffin wis brocht oot

An aa the village stood aroon
Ti sing the psalm
An bid fareweel.
Langsyne an incomer
An noo become their ain

Iss hoose
At saw
Ma faither's grief
At nivver gaed awa
Bit bade aye wi him
Stannin bi the door
Watchin, wytin
Fur ma mither
Bringin hame her eerins.
Syne slowly gaun back
Ti the caul wastelan
O sair reality,
Sittin bi the fire
Alane,
Lanely
Bit nae fur fyowk
Until his ain sair hert
Gied up
Its wyte

Iss hoose
At noo
Is jist a hoose,
Its speerit shiftit on
Ti bide
In o ma hert.

A Floor To Dance On
Sheena Young

CAST:

ALEC HOPE
DOREEN HOPE, his wife
MARGARET HOPE, their daughter
EDDY STEWART, Margaret's boyfriend
TOM MATHERS, a Londoner, newcomer to the area
IRENE MATHERS, his wife
A LAWYER (heard on tape only)

The location is a small coastal village on the Moray Firth, in the North-East of Scotland.

ACTION:

Introduction
Scene One. A year earlier. Alec and Doreen's sitting room.
Scene Two. One month later. A boarding-house.
Scene Three. The next day. Alec and Doreen's sitting room.
Scene Four. The same day. The main room of the house on the hill.
Scene Five. That Friday. At the lawyer's.
Scene Six. Three months later. Alec and Doreen's sitting room.
Scene Seven. The same evening. The main room of the house on the hill.
Scene Eight. Six months later. Alec and Doreen's sitting room.
Scene Nine. The present. The main room of the house on the hill.

PRODUCTION NOTES:

The play has been written to create as few staging problems for the producer as possible. Therefore, it is feasible to imagine it set either on a basic, traditional proscenium arch stage or on the floor of a hall and set in the round.

Apart from four chairs and a small table, no set is essential. However, if something more ambitious is required, there is no reason why a simple set could not be introduced, which could be quickly adapted to the different situations. However, it should not be allowed to become so complicated that it would interfere with the flow from one scene to another.

Similarly, although changes of lighting have been suggested here and there, these could be kept to a simple raising and dimming.

Music is an emotive issue. There are many opportunities for the use of music to enhance the moods. There has been no attempt to suggest particular themes as the area is so subjective. Either old and familiar tunes, of which there are many suitable, or original works could add greatly to the interpretation, but this is a decision best left to the producer.

An interval has been suggested, but this is by no means necessary if it is not appropriate to the venue or the occasion.

Dialect is notoriously difficult to write and spell. While Eddy and Margaret have Banffshire coastal accents, it is only Alec and Doreen who speak the true dialect. Their written speeches have been researched and are authentic, but the spelling of certain words leaves an ambiguity. Experienced actors will have no difficulty coping with the reading.

SCENE 1

A BARE STAGE WHICH WILL LATER BECOME ALEC AND DOREEN'S SITTING ROOM. ALEC ENTERS, CARRYING A SMALL TABLE WHICH HE PLACES CL … FROM HIS POCKET, HE PRODUCES AN EMBROIDERED TABLECOVER WHICH HE SPREADS ON THE TABLE AND CAREFULLY ADJUSTS. ALEC IS IN HIS LATE FIFTIES, A PAWKY MAN, DRESSED LIKE COUNTLESS MALE NORTH-EAST WORTHIES WHO FREQUENT BOWLING GREENS AND HARBOURS OFFERING OPINIONS AND FREE ADVICE TO ANYONE WILLING TO LISTEN OR INDEED ANYONE WHO WILL STAND STILL LONG ENOUGH TO BE ACCOSTED. DURING HIS INTRODUCTORY SPEECH, HE GOES OFF AND BRINGS ON TWO SIMPLE KITCHEN CHAIRS, WHICH HE SETS UP ON EITHER SIDE OF THE TABLE.

ALEC, TO AUDIENCE

Looks like rain. (PAUSE) Nae that we couldna be daein' wi'it. Still, there'll be some that are nae satisfied. Fairmers. They'll nae be pleased. Fairmers are nivir pleased. (HE CHUCKLES) Nae that they hivna hid a lot tae pit up wi considerin the mairkit. Eu-ro-pean, that is. Ae'ways changin things. (HE SITS ON CHAIR, R OF TABLE) A wee bit o' change is a fine thing. Now and again. But ye can nivir tell far it'll lead ye. Even here in the village - ye'd hardly recognise the place wi new folk. Maistly English and Glass-wee-jins. (HE SNIFFS) Same difference. Nae that I'm a racist. Dinna approve o that. Fine folk, maist o them. It's jist that they're nearly a toon folk. An they bring their toon ways o thinkin. An that leads tae mis- understandins an the odd wee problem. An they bring change. (DOREEN ENTERS L, CARRYING A TRAY WITH LITTLE POTS OF PAINT, BRUSHES AND SMALL PLASTIC FOOTBALL FIGURES. SHE SETTLES DOWN IN THE OTHER CHAIR AND STARTS TO PAINT A FIGURE. SHE IS A PLEASANT-LOOKING, MOTHERLY WOMAN WHO KNOWS EXACTLY HOW TO HANDLE THE VARIOUS MEMBERS OF HER FAMILY) Fit is't the nicht, Doreen? The Rangers? Celtic? Ah! (HE NODS SAGELY) The aul strip! (TO AUDIENCE) This is my wife, Doreen. We found oursels last year slap, bang, wallop in the middle o mair change than we'd hid in thirty years o married life. (LIGHTS DIM BUT GRADUALLY RISE. IT IS ONE YEAR EARLIER, DURING THE REST OF THE SPEECH. EDDY AND MARGARET ENTER R, HOLDING HANDS. THEY ARE IN THEIR EARLY TWENTIES, BOTH BRIGHT AND ATTRACTIVE. WHILE THEY BOTH HAVE SCOTS' ACCENTS, THEY DO NOT SPEAK IN THE RICH DIALECT OF THE OLDER GENERATION) That's oor quine, Margaret. Bonny, eh? (HE WINKS AT AUDIENCE) Ye'll nae expect a prize for guessin that she and her braw lad, Eddy, had a bittie news tae pass on. (HE PULLS A P&J FROM HIS POCKET AND, TURNING TO THE FOOTBALL PAGE, STARTS TO READ)

DOREEN (STILL PAINTING, NOT LOOKING UP) Had a nice time, dear? Go an make yourselves some coffee.

ALEC (FROM THE DEPTHS OF THE PAPER) Did ye get the hot dog stand finished?

DOREEN It's nae quite dry, but the grandstand's ready.

ALEC Mak me a cuppa file you're at it, Margaret.

MARGARET In a moment. We've some news for you. (THIS GETS NO RESPONSE) Dad, Mum! Listen! We've got news! (THE PARENTS SIGH AND GIVE HER THEIR FULL ATTENTION) Eddy and me … well, we want to … we're going to start looking for a place of our own.

DOREEN (NOT TOO SURPRISED, RISES AND KISSES THEM BOTH) I canna pretend I'm surprised. Have you fixed a date? Or are ye thinkin o a long engagement?

EDDY (EMBARRASSED) Actually, Mrs Hope, no. We weren't exactly talking about engagements … we were … sort of … going to just …

ALEC (CRUSHING HIS NEWSPAPER) I see! It's goin to be een o those modern affairs, is it? My daughter's tae be a bidey-in!

MARGARET (SOOTHING) No, Dad, it's not like that. It's me that doesn't want to get married. Not yet, anyway. Maybe later - we'll see.

ALEC (STILL ANGRY) An in the meantime, ye'll jist live in sin until ye div decide! (MOCKING) A come-and-go-as-ye-please affair, nae strings attached, nae questions asked!

EDDY No, Mr Hope, we're serious about one another. This is for keeps as far as I'm concerned. (HE REPEATS PLATITUDES HE'S HEARD HERE AND THERE BUT IS QUITE SERIOUS) It's just that we don't see the point of marriage. It's got no place in the nineties. Most people who get married nowadays seem to think more about the wedding than they do about the life they will spend together. Margaret and I can love one another and promise to be faithful without having to sign little bits of paper.

ALEC (SNEERING) And fit about children, hiv ye thocht o that? Ye ken fit a child is withoot that "little bit of paper"? He's a bastard, that's fit he is! Fit are folk gin to say aboot that! Fit'll they say?

MARGARET (CROSSING BEHIND HIM AND PUTTING HER ARMS AROUND HIS NECK) We don't plan any children yet, Dad. It's too soon. There are too many things to be settled first. A house - that'll mean a mortgage. We won't be able to think about children for a long time. And maybe by then (TRYING TO PLEASE HIM) it'll be time to think of a wedding and a cake and flowers and all that!

ALEC Oh, yes, a fite weddin it'll be, ah suppose!

MARGARET (BRIGHTLY) Come into the kitchen, Eddy, and we'll make that coffee! (SHE AND EDDY MOVE TO THE R SIDE OF THE STAGE, SOFTER LIT, WHERE THEY STAND DEEP IN DISCUSSION. ALEC AND DOREEN SIT, STARING INTO THE AUDIENCE. THE NEXT SEQUENCE, LIKE SIMILAR ONES LATER IN THE PLAY, IS DELIVERED IN A STYLIZED MANNER, RATHER LIKE A POEM OR A SONG)

ALEC It seems like yesterday -

DOREEN I'm sure that it was yesterday -

ALEC She fell aff her swing -

DOREEN And broke her tooth

ALEC She grat in my airms

DOREEN She grat in my airms

ALEC Fit a wee darlin

DOREEN She wis bright an cliver

ALEC Ah'd hoped fir a granchild
Maybe two
To sit on ma knee an be
Told stories to

DOREEN She'd look lovely in white
With a full, flowin skirt,

Freesias in her hair!
Ah'd hiv loved to be there!

ALEC A bonny wee girl, who'd
Call me Granpa.
(CHANGES TONE)
Ah've a good bit o wood in the shed.
It'd be good in the shed
To mak a Noah's Ark -
A boat painted red!

DOREEN We'd hae a choir tae sing Bach -
Ah like a bit o Bach.
Lots o champagne tae drink
An "A lighter shade o pale" ah think

ALEC Ma granchild would be called -

DOREEN But all that she will bring -

ALEC Bastard!

DOREEN Shame! (LIGHTS DIM ON ALEC AND DOREEN AND COME UP ON EDDY AND MARGARET IN THE KITCHEN)

EDDY Of course I understand - They're old!

MARGARET I know you understand - Not so very old!

EDDY Ideas that once were tried and true
Have moved and changed, and people do
Quite naturally things which were never done -
Like living together, two as one.
Morals change.

MARGARET But it's hard for them to understand
That this is the life we've hoped

and planned
To lead.
It's hard for them to see us begin
Our lives together in what seems
sin
And greed.
Values change.

(CUT TO BLACK DURING WHICH THE TABLE AND CHAIRS ARE MOVED TO DIFFERENT POSITIONS FOR SCENE 2)

Fiery
John Aberdein

The sma wifie cam ower the weet threshold an hung hir cloaks on a peg.

The hoose wis empty an cauld. The door stude open on the dusky wids, there wis nae thru fae heater nor fridge, but the soon o pulsin wattirs cam roarin up fae the linn.

She turnt an luikit at the wids, stude in the moo o the ha, waitin. The wids were aa tanglit, twiggies an boos o branksome oak, pale leaves a jigsaw on the sodden gress. She waitit, an a shadda detachit fae the trees an cam ower till'r. Far hiv ye been? she spierit.

Tint i the wids aa day cam ees answer. Tint i the wids.

Ee went in the hoose afore hir an she close-haalt the door ahint. Ee wis a broon kinna lad, a straggle o hair, shooders like hoof fungus, lang sable brushes in ees cluik. They went in ben the parlour an stude at the cauld cauld grate. An far hiv ye ben pintin? Fit hiv ye been pintin? Hir airms wis oot the hole o hir gansey, hir sheen kickt aff in the ingle.

Ah tuik the mornin sun tae pint the oak leaves yella.

An?

An orange.

An?

An the rain's made it aa wash oot.

Hir hauns were claspit roon ees waist, ees breeks gone ankleward.

An foo will ye pint me noo that it's aa gone dark?

Ah'll licht us a fire.

Wi fit?

Wi fittivver comes tae haun.

The man at'll pint me true is nivver feart tae combust ees auld brushes.

She frottit a spunk an ees auld brushes went stracht tae the back o the fire, a lowe o crimsie, blue, sienna. Ees auld barkit claes were next. She wis nakit afore'm.

An foo will ye earn a kiss fae ma lips?

Yir lips are aa fite!

Willna ye kiss them then?

Aye but.

Aye but fit, bonny widman?

Aye but Ah'm feart ye'll tak aa ma colour.

She pullit the widman intae hir bosie, ee wis auld noo an crackly.

Na, na lad, jist ben tae ma will, ye'se hae colour yet.

An she plunkit'm doon on the widden cheer, an rode'm tae bits, tae feed the new fire.

The vind begood tae rise, tirl at the winda an sing in the lum. She harkent tae that singin, an wi a sudden doonracht o winter, intae the room cam smaik an a man. Ee wis hissin an hummin fae ees time in the lum.

Can ye sing me a sang o nae snaa an nae rain?

Ah can sing ye a sang o snaa an syne rain.

Can ye sing me a dry sang, warm at the fire?

Ah can sing ye a sang o strang tempest an ire.

A man canna sing better, ee maun feed ma fire.

An she tuuik the lum-traiveller an lay on'm hertily, lowsin ees sowl fae the pech o ees lungs, pittan'm singin back in the fire.

Noo she wandert arron the room, pickan at the libraire shelfs, blawin stoor an thumbin throu the auld queer quairs. Duino, The White Goddess, Morgan le Fay, they were aa there. Fitna pooers were hirs gin she culdna read? Fitna blitheness wis hirs gin she culdna hae a poet clappin lips till hir lug? Fitna poem wis even fit for sicna deep deep lug?

Serve me! she cried tae the shelfs an a whisp o stoor tuik shap as a lang strang mannie.

Ah'll serve ye quo the mannie, an quotit yerds of ballatrie till'rr, up agin the lang wa.

Serve me proper! cried the wifie, fingerin ees neck.

Ah'll gie ye proper lauchit the manie, an quotit screeds o bawdrie, till the hail hoose gaed shakkin.

Nae anither wird ye scunner! cryit the wife at lest, hurlin hir hair aboot clean dement, as she thrawit ees thrapple like an auld dune cockrel, waitin ees turn on midden or fire.

This mannies nooadays wis nae muckle eese. She lay doon at the hearthside, streekin hir lang back tae the libraire wa, hir bosoms curvit like twa munes tae the bleezin fire. Hir hanch stude prood, hir chowk begood tae saften, hir skin wis baith schaddowit an gowden.

She wis dry, she wis warm. Lat wattirs roar. Wi shutten een she dwaamt o fire aye-jiggin: upheatin the earth aneath hir, blawin throu tall calm winds.

Release
Anne McCabe

Let a tear
Drop
Into the river
Flow
To the ocean
Wave
To the water
Fall
Through the ice
Break.

January Storm
Anne McCabe

The sea is on edge and wants out.
Restlessly she turns in her bed:
Waves need away.

The sea is on edge and wants out.
Ferociously she spits salt on wounds;
The world.

An excerpt from a long story in Scots ...

Far's The Marischal?

William Buchan

CHAPTER 1

"But Jimmy, fit are we supposed to work the fairm wi, if you winna gie us the bit for oor tractor?"

"At's your problem. At's your problem. You twa are ae the same. I'm still wytin for ye ti square up yer last bill."

Jimmy Simpson wis stannin his grun because Doddie and Robbie Milne were the bane o his life. They were ae comin ti his garage for bits for their aul' tractor, but gettin ony money oot o them wis a different maitter a' thegither.

"Aye and fit wye are we supposed ti pey ye, fan we canna get onything oot o the grun because wir tractor's broken?"

"Like I said; at's your problem. The bits are here fan ye've got the money for 'em. Noo, it's sax o'clock and I'm deen for the nicht. I've got a big day the morn so, come on, on yer wye, on yer wye. Come back on Monday if ye've got the money."

The twa loons were ushered oot o the garage still tryin ti argue the pynt. But it wis nae eese. Jimmy wis a man o principle. And it wis principally money he wis interested in, so Doddie and Robbie had nae chunce o winnin iss particular debate.

Doddie and Robbie were twins born and brocht up on the Knockenhill fairm jist ootside Peterheid. Apairt fae Robbie haen dark hair fan Doddie wis fair and being aboot six inches shorter than Doddie, they were almost the marra. Ye couldna tell them apairt fan ye were three mile awa.

"Fit are we gaan ti dee, Dod?" asked Robbie. "We need at tractor ti get thon last twa parks turned ower iss wick-en."

"Aye Robbie I ken, but at hungry brute's nae gaan ti gie us the bit til we've the siller for it. A' that he's worryin aboot is his big day the morn. Nivver mind aboot ither folks"

"I'd like ti mak a minneer o his wik-en like he's deen ti oors, the great fat stirk!" Doddie went on.

"Aye, sae would I. Fit wye does he keep sayin things twice? At's queer at."

The twa brithers sat a filey on the wa' ootside the garage and mulled ower fit they would like ti dee ti Jimmy.

Suddenly Dod's een lichted up.

"Robbie, I've got a richt idea for gettin wir ain back on Jimmy. Come on, we need ti get Airchie ti gies a han. I'll tell ye a' aboot it on the wye doon the road."

So the twins heided aff ti fin oot if their cousin Airchie Pirie wis hame fae the quarry yet.

CHAPTER 2

The morning sun wis streamin in the bedroom windae as Jimmy Simpson slowly opened his een. He dozed for a puckle minutes before his brain kicked inti gear and he realised fit day it wis. He gave his wife Thelma a shak but she only turned ower ti her ither side athoot even brakkin oot o her snore.

"Ye jist canna get weemin ti tak things seriously," thocht Jimmy ti himsel as he louped oot o his bed and shuffled inti his slippers.

This indeed wis a big day for oor Jimmy. Ye see, James Campbell Simpson Esquire, apart fae being a pillar o industry in Peterheid wis also the Provost. And today, Baron Von Cashenburger and his wife were peyin an official visit ti the toon ti unveil a new statue o ane o Peterheid's heroic sons, "Marischal Keith".

Marischal Keith wis ane o the Keith family, fa were the Lord Marischals o Scotland and they bid in Inverugie Castle, jist three miles oot o Peterheid. The Marischal had been a sojer twa'r three hunner eer ago and by a' accoonts had been a bit o a hero in battles ower in Germany afore snuffin it near the Baron's hame toon. The statue had been a present ti Peterheid fae the folk in Germany, as a mark o their respect. At least it wis better than the last presents wi got fae the Germans. They flattened the picter hoose. Aifter being delivered a fortnicht ago, it wis stood on a granite block jist ootside the toon hoose at the tap o Broad Street. It's verra likely that the folk o Peterheid hadnae even noticed iss great lump o steen. Mind you, if ye came hame stottin drunk ae nicht, ye could guarantee that plenty o folk would hiv seen ye. Peterheid folk didna miss a thing as lang as it wis something they could ca' somebody for.

But iss mornin the Marischal would hae a reed velvet curtain thrown ower him, jist wytin for the Baron ti pull the string and condemn oor hero for ever ti look doon the length o Broadgate. Mind you he did stan wi his airm pyntin straicht oot at the British Legion Club bar. The Legion committee couldnae believe a' this free advertisin!

Jimmy wasted nae time in washin and shavin and, aifter finally managin ti get Thelma oot o her bed ti mak his brakfist, set aboot puttin on his fresh sark and good suit. Aifter preening himsel in front o the mirror for a good ten minutes, he went doon stairs for his usual ham and eggs wi a' the trimmins. Ye didna get ti be a fine figure o a man like Jimmy athoot fulling yer face at every opportunity.

"Richt Thelma, richt Thelma, I'm awa doon ti the toon hoose ti mak sure a'thing's tickety-boo afore the Baron comes. He's nae due afore three o'clock so I've got a fyle yet ti see that a'thing's OK and dee a bitty o my paperwork fan I'm wytin. We're gaan roon ti the Palace Hotel aifter the ceremony for a buffet, so I'll get a couple o pies fae the bakers for my denner. I'll put a taxi up for ye aboot twa o'clock, twa o'clock. So mak sure yer ready, mak sure yer ready. Oh, and dinna put on yon hat ye wore the last time. We couldna get moved for starlins and sparra's at day."

Drivin doon Queen Street in the sunshine, Jimmy thocht that this wis the life he wis born for. Weerin the Provost's gold chains and official robes, meetin a' these foreign dignitaries, photos in the paper and slap up denners in the toon's best hotels. J.C. Simpson wis as happy wi' life as ye could be athoot winnin the pools. Nae that Jimmy needed money. His garage had been started by his faither eers ago. At that time aul' Jimmy wis also the toon's undertaker. Fan he deet they beeried him themsels so as naebody else made a profit oot o it. Young Jimmy, being the only loon, took ower the business fan iss happened, but he wisnae keen on the burial side o things so he sellt a' the gear and bocht a new ramp for the garage. Puttin em doon ae minute and puttin em up the next so ti spik. But the thing that abody noticed aboot Jimmy wis that he had iss awfa habit o sayin things twice. Some folk said iss wis hereditary because his faither wis a dummy, but I dinna ken.

Aye, Jimmy wis like a king in a royal cairrage as he drove doon Queen Street in his blue vanny. He even gave twa folk that were stannin on the corner newsin, a richt royal wave. As he drove past the toon hoose ti park the van, he thocht that there wis somethin different aboot the toon iss mornin. He wunnered if it wis the bonny sunshine (maist unusual in Peterheid) that made things look different. Mair than likely it wis the scaffies that had been oot early and swiped up the mess that would hiv been left fae last nicht. Fit ivver it wis, he couldna put his finger on't. But he wisnae bothered aboot it. Naething wis gaan ti spyle iss day.

CHAPTER 3

Miss McRobbie, the cooncil clerkess, wis already at her desk fan Jimmy entered his office. Biddy McRobbie had worked for the cooncil for nearly forty eer. Some folk thocht that she wis mairriet ti the cooncil. She certainly hadna managed ti find a bloke a' this eers. Mind ye, wi that nose...but at's a different story. The fact wis that Miss McRobbie wis the cooncil. She bid in a wee flat jist oot the back fae the toon hoose and spent maist o her time in the office. There wis nae cooncil business that went on that Biddy didna ken aboot. That iss wis a Saiturday didna maiter ti her. There wis something gaan on so she had ti be ere.

"Aye, aye Biddy, fit a bonny morning it is," said Jimmy cheerily.

"It is, Provost but ye're lang the day."

There's nae doot fa wis the boss here. Jimmy had jist gotten his starn en' inti the big cheer ahin the desk fan Miss McRobbie put a heap o letters in front o him.

"You better see ti at afore ye dee onything else," she said and walked oot.

Jimmy shook his heid. "I wush at wummin would retire or fin a man for hersel," he thocht. Fit ivver wis different iss mornin it certainly wisna the dragon ben the hoose. He got up and took his jacket aff ti hing up on the coatstan in the corner. The sunshine streamed in the windae and Jimmy couldna resist a quick look oot ower his empire. Ye could see ower the hairbour ti the sea ahin it. Leadin fae the hairbour wis Broad Street itsel. He looked fae the bottom o the street, up past the Reform Monument and continued up ower the public carpark ti the steps o the toon hoose itsel, far the statue o Marischal Keith stood a' happit wi his bonny reed curtain.

At that split second, rigor mortis seemed ti strike Jimmy. A'thing froze except for his moo fit jist opened and shut like a goldfish withoot ony soon comin fae it. His face grew reeder and reeder until it looked as if his heid would burst. Suddenly, as though somebody had jist pressed a button, he turned and bolted through to Miss McRobbie's office.

"Biddy, Biddy," he shouted, "Far is it? Far is it?"

"Stop sayin a'thing twice Provost. Fit is it ye've lost?"

Jimmy wis hae'n kittins by this time. "Me, me, I hivnae lost onything. Far is it? Far is it?" he went on pyntin ti the windae.

"Calm yersel doon Provost. Fit on earth are ye on aboot." Miss McRobbie finally got up fae her desk and went ower ti the windae. "I canna see onything".

"See, see, I tellt ye, I tellt ye. It's awa. It's awa," he blurted.

"Fit's awa? I canna see onything."

This wis too much for Jimmy and he somehow managed ti stagger ower ti the windae and pynt. "Are you blin wummin? Can ye nae see? It's nae ere! Far's the Marischal? Far's the Marischal?"

At this Jimmy sank inti a kind o semi-coma on the leather cooch in the office.

"Fit am I gaan ti dee?" he wailed, "Fit am I gaan ti dee?"

"Well stop sayin' a'thin twice for a start. At gets on my nerves," Biddy snapped unsympathetically.

But Biddy McRobbie had nivver seen the Provost in a state like iss afore. He wis oot o his heid wi' drink at the cooncil Christmas doo twa eer ago but he wisna as bad as iss.

"Will I gie the doctor a phonny?" she asked

This started Jimmy again. "The doctor, the doctor. Fit eese is a doctor ti the Marischal? Yer nae bloomin wise you."

Biddy could see that things were gettin worse fast. "At's it then," she said "I'll phone the bobbies."

Chapter 4

The phone rang in the police office jist as Sergeant Angus Buchan feenished stirrin his tae. He muttered a puckle oaths afore pickin up the receiver and announcin in his best police vyce, "Good morning, Peterheid Police Station."

Biddy McRobbie's vyce came doon the line at him. "Is 'at the Police? Iss is the cooncil here, pit me on ti the Chief Coonstable."

Angus recognised the vyce and wushed that he had jist ignored the ringin phone and feenished his tae. He'd a funny feeling that his taebreak wis ower and deen wi noo.

"Ah, Miss McRobbie, the Chief Constable disna mak a habit o coomin oot here on a Saiturday mornin so if yer sair seekin ti spik til im ye'll need ti phone Aiberdeen." He seriously dooted if there wis actually a phone on the Balgownie golf coorse. "Iss is Sergeant Buchan here, can I help ye?" he asked as politely as he could.

"Well there's naethin wrang wi me, but ye better get ower here quick and see the Provost afore he gings doolally."

"Verra well, Miss McRobbie, I'll be ower i noo." Angus hung up the phone and wunnered fit wis wrang noo. He kent aboot the Baron's visit iss aifterneen. In fact he had twa specials fae Longside and Mintlaw coming doon at denner time jist ti make it look mair official. There wis nae real need for ony extra police but it wis ae overtime for the lads and a good chunce ti hae a newsie and a couple o drams wi aul' freens.

As seen as Angus Buchan came roon the corner ti the front o the toon hoose, his highly trained policeman's ee spotted that the half-ton statue o Marischal Keith wisna far it wis supposed ti be. He had a terrible feelin that this wis gaan ti be a day ti myn on for a lang time.

He entered the cooncil office ti find the Provost streetched oot on the cooch deein a good impression o a flukie that had been washed up on the san. Miss McRobbie was dichtin his foreheid wi a cloot.

"Mornin Provost, Miss McRobbie. Far's the Marischal?"

At this, Vesuvius erupted again. "Far's the Marischal? Far's the Marischal? At's fit you're ower here ti fin' oot, ye neep," screamed Jimmy Simpson. "Fit am I gan ti dee? Fit am I gan ti dee?"

Miss McRobbie tried ti calm him and managed ti get him back on ti the cooch.

"There noo, Provost. Calm doon. Try breathin slowly".

"Try nae breathin at a'," thocht Angus.

"Does he ae say a'thin twice?" asked the bobby.

Eventually Angus managed ti get the full story oot o them. Apparently, sometime between the oors o ten o'clock on Friday nicht and sax o'clock on Saiturday morning, Marischal Keith had been kidnapped! And by the look o the Provost, if the Marischal wisna fun seen, there micht be a body ti be dealt wi as well.

"Richt en, I think I've gotten a' the details. I'll awa ti the station an start makin enquiries."

"And hing in, hing in!" shouted Jimmy as the bobby left the office.

CHAPTER 5

There wis only twa'r three places in Peterheid ye could rely on ti hear a' the latest gossip or scandal. There wis the bingo hally but at wisna open at this time o the mornin; the pubs, but again it wis a bit early for 'em, although nae doot, there would be the usual crowdy sittin haen their "mornin" in the Royal bar across the road. Thirdly, there wis the mission at the hairbour, far a' the fishermen went for their tae. Angus decided ti try the mission first. This wisna because o any special police technique but because he still hidna heen his cuppy o tae himsel yet.

"Hello Sergeant Buchan. Fit can we get ye the day?" asked Meggie the mission wifie.

"Oh jist a mug o tae, wi a wee suppy milk but nae suger, ta."

The policeman took his tae ower ti a table aside the windae far Charlie Mac wis sittin reading the Press and Journal.

"Aye, aye Charlie, fit like?"

"Oh my God. I'm jist landed fae the sea iss mornin. I hinna heen time ti dee onything yet, Sergeant." Charlie's colour drained as the policeman sat doon.

Angus lauched, "I didna think ye had Charlie. But I seen ye sittin here and I jist wunnered if ye'd seen the Marischal?"

"The Marischal," Charlie shook his heid slowly. "Na, I've nivver seen it. Hiv ye tried young Cheesy aboord the boat? He watches a' that cowboy films."

The Sergeant explained that he wisna interested in a cowboy film but in the disappearance o a statue. This confused Charlie even mair, "Govey Dicks. Hiv ye tried the museum? There wis statues in ere the last time I wis in."

Angus could see that he wisna makin ony progress here, so he jist feenished his tae athoot raivellin the man ony further.

On his wye back up Broad Street, the Sergeant decided ti put his theory ti the test and see fa wis a' in the Royal bar at iss time o the mornin. He kent that there wis nae pynt o gaan ti the front door o the pub because Sandy McIver the barman wouldna open the door ti onybody afore openin time. A' the trade conducted ootside licensin oors wis deen through the back door. Angus didna bother knockin as he walked inti the bar. Sandy wis washin doon the coonter and, as predicted by the bobby, ower in the corner, twa o Peterheid's finest exponents o the art o excessive drinkin were deep in discussion aboot Aiberdeen's match this aifterneen.

Sandy jumped when he saw the policeman, "Sergeant? Fit can a dee for ye? Come on you twa ower ere. Hurry up and feenish cleaning up at neuk. The boys are jist gien me a han iss mornin fan I wisnae feelin great."

"I can see fine fit at twa's deein but I'm here on mair serious business. Div ony o ye ken fit happened ti the Marischal last nicht?"

"I hivna heard aboot it. Fit happened til im?" asked the barman.

Yet again the policeman explained that the statue had geen missin.

Sandy shouted ower ti the drunks in the corner, "The Sergeant's lookin for the Marischal. Div ye ken onything aboot it?"

Tommy Strachan couldna resist haen a bit o fun wi the bobby. "Div ye hear at Bobo. The sherriff's lookin for his marshal."

Bobo Robertson kechled, "Hiv ye tried the OK Coral Sergeant? I heard there wis a gunfecht ere last nicht."

Angus's face grew darker and the twa drunks thocht that maybe they'd geen a bitty ower far.

"You twa had better myn at ye're nae supposed ti be in here. I could hae ye up, ye ken." He turned ti the barman. "And you better myn that I'm on the licensin boord, the next time ye're up for renewal."

This wis a bit o a show o poower fae Angus. He kent he could chuck 'em oot but they would jist ging somewye else. They were'na deein ony hairm and at least they were'na moochin aff o onybody. But he had ti keep up appearances.

There wis naethin else but ti ging back ti the station and plan his next move ...

Observance

Ian Morrison

On a fat-tyred three-wheeled ATB
a boy and a girl speed around a field
on a cold but clear-skied early March morning.

The girl perches on the small black back seat
her hands tight clutching each other round
the boy's chest, her eyes and open mouth spread wide

with the thrill and fear. The collar of his new
two-tone-dark-blue-and-fluorescent-pink
Nevica is her focus, her respite

from the kaleidoscope they make of the ground's
rushing, threadbare, dull-green-and-earth surface.
From neighbouring fields the cattle chew and stare

between crops. Their indifference is mild,
they scratch largely acquiescent backsides
against leaning, archaic grey-barked fenceposts.

The pair scream close by as I walk past the new
landscaped pond, tramping down the gentle slope
towards the Deveron, encased rod in hand,

feeling the yield and spring in the soft black loam
turned forever by the wide-slabbed tyre treads.
Their cries and laughter ululate in the breeze.

From somewhere, above the noise I hear an
oystercatcher's cry, then catch its orange beak
against the dark background of the dense firs

on the other river bank. The flies will soon
dance above the water; rippling trout breaths
will shortly lure the synthetic-tufted hook.

Autumn

Ian Morrison

The dun stubble, the thinning foliage,
the faded greens and yellows of the remaining grass,
the clanking pirouettes of the eight-socked

reversible ploughs, the renewed fencing
ringing its tautness when climbed over, the black
crows hopping across the narrow, puddled roads

towards the somethings they have seen and are
hurrying to eat, the one roe I've seen all year
breaking cover to run, with such balance,

across the small fields sloping towards
the silver curve of the grey sea's horizon,
the thickening glaur, the dense seagull sweeps

of the harvested potato parks,
dimming whins, rusting ferns, the ditchwater
frothed, and smoky with leaking silage bree,

the tractors' bouncing whine on the roads, the
toned grey skies, the never-clean dogs worrying
the tyres of the car as we drive past

smallholdings strewn with disintegrating
implements, smoke, pale firewood, dull sun,
the shifted earth, the harvesting by spotlight.

Observations

Ian Morrison

The sun shadows the land behind the grey sky:
the arctic wind sweeps the drills clawed raggedly
on the rolling hill: the topsoil has drifted

on the ice. Much else would be white ‑ the gnawed
neeps like apple cores, the staring sheep, the hoared
weeds manic in the wind. However,

above all else, there's silence: the flat blade
of the wind has beaten life from the day.
I walk past the house and farm signs opening

and closing towards me, signing history
of the land: Sol Y Mar, Greenfield, Easter
Howemoss, Mulberry Manor. Black pennants

of torn plastic fly from the barbed wire fences:
the signs' letters are red against the black iron.
A mashed seagull's wings flap uselessly

on the road. Stamping my frozen feet, they
tap hard on the frozen earth. Our bereftness
echoes (but quietly) over the set aside.

The Poet-Pen and The Preacher
Greg Dawson Allen

As an old man of eighty-six years, the Rev. John Skinner is sadly preparing to leave Linshart, his home at Longside, Aberdeenshire. Still grieving the loss of Grizzel, his beloved wife who died some six years previously, Skinner is packing his belongings into a trunk to begin the journey to Aberdeen to live with his son, knowing that he will never see Longside again.

On the 16th June 1807, four days after arriving at his son's house, the much respected poet and preacher died, "Without a struggle or a sigh".

In this extract, Skinner recalls his childhood and first steps as a young schoolmaster in the parish of Monymusk, Aberdeenshire.

❖

SKINNER I began in this warld wi nithing bit my birthday claes an it is certain that I'll cairy nithing oot!

I've teen o late tae thinking back tae my bairnheed an my first mither, Jean. The first an last tae be teen frae her wyme, a bairgin mite, filling my lungs wi the Birse air ... an the reek frae the burning peat in the ingle. Happit an waarm sooking frae the pap ... a hairmless geet.

Nae seener wis I crawlin than I heez'd up on my ain twa spawls an held gaun wi sic a virr. It wis aft said, ee'n then, that wee Jockie Skinner hid a mind o his ain.

WOMAN
{singing old children's rhyme}
There wis twa doggies,
An they gaed tae the mill,
An they got a lick oot o this wifie's pyock,
An anither oot o the neesht wifie's pyock,
An a leb oot o the dam,
An syne they geed hame,
Loupie for loup, loupie for loup.

SKINNER The lauchin wis replaced by the greetin o faither. I wis daumer't wi fit happened. "Teen tae sleep till the trump soons," faither said. Bit I niver sa mither Jean again. My hairt wis as sair then as it is noo wi a pain I've growin tae be familiar wi.

A Mother! {Ah, the venerable name,
Which my young lips were never taught to frame},
She, whose warm bowels form'd my infant span.

The hoosie at Balfour an the wids o Birse were left ahin as faither bunnel'd his grief alang wi the kists an a frichted bairn intae a cairt an hurl'd the puckle miles tae the paris o Echt. Syne there wis anither knee tae be dirl'd on an in atween squeel an sleep they gaed me a gaggle o brithers an sisters. Faither wis baith parent an dominie, instructing me tae'wards Knox an Presbyterianism a stepping stane frae becoming a dominie like himsel tae the poopit o a paris kirk an respectibility. That wis something that he niver askit bit earned roon aboot for nae ither dominie sent mair loons tae university than John Skinner the elder.

I wis hardly thirteen fan I wis pit for'ad as a candidate for the annual bursery competition for entry tae Marischal College. A translation o English prose intae Latin wis nae tuilzie for a loon that heard as muckle Latin spoken in the hoose as ony pupil o Virgil or Livy.

That wis eneuch tae allow me tae follow in the fitsteps o anither son o Birse, Doctor Ramsey, fa the college owed his posthumous generosity, an lay mysel open tae the mony influences an reerie of the college, the likes o wis niver kent in the paris squeel. I wis behuddin tae faither for his teachings bit this wis riches beyond comprehension.

Studies in Medicine, Botany, Latin, Greek, Divinity, Philosophy - Euclid's elements and Aristotle's De Anima, De Poetica an Rhetoric - there wis as many opinions an hypotheses as there were professors tae utter them! Manna tae stech the mind an soul!

November tae April wis the sowing o the seed - May tae October the hairst o learning reaped by the bairns in kintra squeels through us being pit oot tae turn theory intae practice.

Fower 'eer later aifter boo'in oot as a scarlet robed member o the Magistrand class I spadd'it oot ower the Stocket-Heed for Kemnay tae tak up my first charge as assistant dominie.

Kemnay gaed me siller in my pooch bit Monymusk opened gates tae fields o reapers croon'd wi corn. "The earth brought forth vegetation, plants yielding seed according to their own kinds, and trees bearing fruit in which is their seed, each according to its kind. And God saw that it was good." I call it paradise on Donside!

The maister poet, Alexander Pope, wis seen as a prodigy at siventeen. I'm achteen an struggling like the loon David aneath the birn o Saul's armour tae scratch oot my ain rhymes. In atween yokin the interest o the geets in the squeel an the sweet Goddess o the lyre tae inspire my quill tae flow like Pope's there wis aye beauties tae tak the ee o a beardless, Protestant dominie.

Monymusk wis a Garden o Eden wi young blooming floors ready for the pickin - only I wis as much an apprentice wi the fair quines as I wis wi versifying! To me how happy would minute prove, Were I the object of Fair Rachel's love!

Bit the position o assistant tae the dominie wis held in nae sma asteem. Gentry an tenants welcomed me intae their boorichies. Maiters o kintra or craft were discussed an I wis weel aquint wi baith an could haud my ain amid the shirran'n that oft wis roust'd atween cankart chiels.

For a bit loon I could be as contarmachious as Pope fitch brocht me mair than a puckle o heez'd ee-bro's an fool glowers. Aifter a, wis I nae responsible for their bairn's leerin an spiritual upbringing - an were these nae the swankies o the paris?

The opinions o the dominie hid tae echo those o the great mannies o literature an theological stunnin, nae a primpit ill-hadden ghaist as them that aye deev'd on the loodist thocht. I'll soochin a joog wi fa'iver will hae my company - Lillie's best ale or a skelp o wine. For maist in an aroon Monymusk I wis a the mair respected for gab'in my ain mine! An especially be Miss Potts, the Lady Grant an her husband, the lairdskip, Sir Archibald. Ah, the Lady Bountiful o the district, the darling mither tae bonnie lassies - an the possessor o the finest library ootside o Marischal College!

This play was premiered at the Edinburgh Fringe in 1996.

.....Meanwhile, over at the E.S.O.
Bill Sluyter

.....and I'm standing here on Castle Street, Banff, on a blustery August day. I'm outside the local Employment Service Office and there's a queue that would do justice to a Deveronvale home game. The doors are now opening. Who is first in? It's the girl who worked for a period with Buchan Meat then Grampian Country Chickens and now wants to pack it in (get it?) and work with free-range hens down in The Cotswolds. Best of luck, Emmanuelle. Up at the Signing On desk a regular flourishes the pen with the air of a veteran. Sheer professionalism, I must say. Goodness me, he's finished already! The speed at which some of these Banffie's work (or not) takes my breath away. Two people meander upstairs for the six monthly interview. They're obviously in no hurry having been through this rigmarole before, probably every six months since 1985.

A stout woman approaches the Queries desk and asks if there are any vacancies for a fashion model. The Interviewer giggles girlishly and says, "Ye hinna' a snaba's chance in hell." Brutal and to the point. Brings back memories of the demise of the Soviet Union.

Out of the corner of my eye I can see the Manager chat up the latest staff recruit. Busy, busy, busy these people, always on the go, trying hard to find jobs for people who socially they wouldn't be seen dead with.

Back at the Signing On desk a brouhaha is developing. The client is explaining that she definitely signed on a fortnight ago and the fraught lady behind the desk is insisting she didn't. Takes me back to the time I interviewed Imelda Marcos about how many pairs of shoes she actually possessed. The confrontation is coming to a head when the customer head butts her interviewer. Reminds of the Mike Tyson/Buster Douglas title fight.

A brief hiatus occurs. Tea or coffee time for the beleaguered staff. Out of the corner of my other eye I witness the Manager take a swig at a hip flask. Wise move, I'd say.

Suddenly my personal walkie-talkie buzzes. Macduff has been washed away by a freak tidal wave so I've to hot-foot it across the Deveron and see if there's any sign of life. Who said that reporting about life in Banff and Buchan District is dull and uninteresting?

January 1995
Alex Smith

Sunday - 1
A a day lang strong North win did blaw,
An intae us it did blaw a puckle sna,
The win wis seventy mile the oor or mair,
Intae a storm on the first we div stare.

Monday - 2
Atween the dyke wi fyte wis foo,
A winter wonderlan we see jist noo,
Noo an again a fyte shoor or twa,
At least the win it disnae blaw.

Tuesday - 3
Gless awa doon past minus twal,
afa fine day bit man it's cauld.

Wednesday - 4
Atween the thaw an atween the frost,
Dry, wi winter in oor minds uppermost.

Thursday - 5
A gale force win oot throo the nicht,
The sna's awa a richt welcome sicht,
Day turns oot afa mild an braw,
Ahin the dyke sits doon the sna.

Friday - 6
A fer bit o frost throo the nicht,
A cauld day bit fine an bricht.

Saturday - 7
A hard fyte frost jist like sna,
Sooth win intae us dis blaw.

Sunday - 8
Nae neen like first day o the year,
frost like sna on the grun disappear

Later on atween the frost and thaw,
Jist afore the rain it begins tae fa.

Monday - 9
Wid it rain or wid it nae,
Became fule an weet durin the day,
Be efterneen ere's a richt icy blast,
Gale force win oot o the Wast.

Tuesday - 10
It wis cauld an bare a a day lang,
Shoors o' sleet frae the day began.

Wednesday - 11
Twa inch o sna fin we div rise,
It wis afa cauld at wis nae surprise,
En as the day wears on be the oor,
Noo an again ere's anither wintry shoor.

Thursday - 12
Throo the nicht the sna dis disappear,
Cauld an bare is the day I fear,
En tae wards nicht er's twa inch o sna,
Noo is day I didnae like it ata.

Friday - 13
Nae ony sna the day is fine an dry,
Touch o frost, nae cloods in the sky,
A a at eence gale force wis dis rise,
Wi shoors o sleet fit a surprise.

Saturday - 14
It's win chill says the mannie on TV,
Afa afa cauld oh sae richt wis he.

Sunday - 15
Richt cauld Sooth win it dis blaw,
I hae my doots an forecast sna.

Monday - 16
Still the Sooth win it dis persist,
Tae pit on winter claes I maun insist,
Sleet shoors the worst I ivver sa,
An efter at win it dis gang an fa.

Tuesday - 17
A gey hard frost an Sooth win dis blaw,
Cauldest day ere's been, nae ony eese ata.

Wednesday - 18
Echty mile the oor gales oot throo the nicht,
An afa damage nae a welcome sicht,
Still strong Sooth win it dis blaw awa,
Throo a flurry or twa o some weet sna.

Thursday - 19
Win his drappit doon nae near sae strong,
A touch o frost an cauld were set upon.

Friday - 20
Afa cauld bit fine an dry,
Tae keep oorsels warm we div try.

Saturday - 21
Frosty mornin afa cauld an bare
Sooth win on us wis gey sair,
Win' gale force be the efterneen,
Blaws throo sleet, tae the been.

Sunday - 22
Strong Sooth win' blaws throo rain an sleet,
Withoot a doot the day is fule an weet.

Monday - 23
Sooth win is gale force eence mair,

Blows sleet an sna intae us gey sair,
In the efterneen the win it dis fa,
Ere's a weak bit o sin it wis sae braw.

Tuesday - 24
A cauld day bit oh sae fine,
Bides dry an quate a a the time.

Wednesday - 25
It wull be sna said the mannie on TV,
An sna we did waken up an see.

Thursday - 26
Doon past minus fower gans the gless,
Mair shoors o sna a a day we face.

Friday - 27
A coverin o sna fin we div rise,
Ere's a hard frost at's nae ony surprise,
I aye keep lookin at a strange sky,
The sna starts tae fa yon sleekit wye.

Saturday - 28
Twa fit o sna, bit it dis turn fresh,
Poors o rain en mair sna, fit a mess.

Sunday - 29
A cauld bare win wi a shoor or twa o sna
The sna his sat doon jist winnae gang awa.

Monday - 30
Anither coverin o sna oot throo the nicht,
A richt hard frost warp oorsels up ticht.

Tuesday -31
Throo the nicht gale force win again,
Alang wi at afa heavy shoors o rain,
Dry bit damp at's the day tae be,
Sna' sits doon nae gweed for the e'e.

Daylicht Robbery

Marjory Nicholson

The pyoules o' Peterheid
Stamp on i' reef
An' skrach as they
Rin their ain riot.
A protected species
They pillage an'
Scavenge the land
O' their birth.
The Mafia o' the lums
Wanner at will
An' shite an' skirl
In contempt
If onybody daurs
Tae conter em.
They lach an' yell
At wifies
Hingin oot their
Washin an' fire
At i' sheets
As i' back door shuts.
Wis it ony winner
Big Dod took i'
Law intil 'es ain
Haun an' catapulted
I' thievin vratch
'At jinkit doon
An' nabbit 'es
Bag o' brakkfast
Bacon fin 'e turned
'Es back tae crack
A yarrie intae the pan.

Tattie Howkin'

Angus MacDonald

Div'e ye mind gaen tattie howkin fan ye got time aff the skweel,
Hopin that the digger wid brackdoon ilka second dreel
Ye'r back wis sair fae a that bowin up an doon,
An the cauld damp earth fairly made yer fingirs dirl an stoon,
Ye'd gaither up yer tatties tae try tae beat yer chums,
Bit fan ye look'it up they hid feenish'd an wir sittin on their bums,
At denner time wi clarty han's yer piece ye tried tae eat,
Bit yer body wis sae sair a ower it nearly gaar'd ye greet,
Sine nicht time cam aroon' is it aye dis withoot fail,
An aff hame ye'd gaed wi a bilin o tatties in yer pail,
Fir a the hard work that ye did ye wisna paid a lot,
Sair fingirs an a gey sair back wis the maist thing that ye got,
They hae machines noo that picks the spuds, an files bags them as weel
Aye the bairns noo hiv a better time than fin we were at the skweel,
Bit it nivver did us ony herm that twa weeks o sheer hard graft,
Yet I files think fan we wir young we must hiv been a daft.

A Buchan Winter

Angus MacDonald

The win comes howlin fae the North nippin lugs wi its icy blast,
Tellin ye that winter's caam an simmer time his past,
Trees stanin gaunt an leafless wi branches pintin tae the sky,
An fae the fields comes the soond o the teuchat's langsome cry,
The girss broon an curled up lyin dormant till the Spring,
Cauld winter's fingirs tak's a grip on ilka livin' thing,
The hungry birds scran the hedges fir berries, nuts an the like,
Nae worms fir them, jist wee beasties that hide in some auld dyke,
Days are short an the nichts are dark an lang,
An it's gey slippery underfit nae maiter far ye gaan,
Chappit lips, the Flu, noses rinnin like a waal,
An abody pits the blame on the wither bein sae caul,
Icicles hingin' fae the eaves, frost on the windie pane,
Ice thick on the watter trouchs as hard as granite stane,
The hills a roon are fite wi sna, wi a chance o gettin mair,
Aye faan it comes tae winter, Buchan fair gets its shair.

CONTRIBUTORS' NOTES:
BREAKING NEW GROUND

John Aberdein

From Aberdeen, lives in Orkney. Author of The Can-Can, Ken [Clocktower Publications]

Brian Adams

A Buchan playwright and amateur stage director. Lives in Strichen.

Greg Allen

Playwright, from Aberdeen, lives in Fyvie.

Morag Bisset

Playwright living near Turriff.

Charles Brown

Lives near Banff.

George Bruce

From Fraserburgh, widely-published poet and author.

Tom Bryan

Writer in residence for Banff and Buchan and Aberdeenshire, 1994-1997.

Bill Buchan

A native of Peterhead, writes poetry and stories in his native Doric.

Stuart Campbell

From Lanark, lives near Aberchirder and works in Banff. Musician and mountaineer.

Ian Crockatt

From Perth, works in Banff. Widely published poet.

James Duthie

Has written plays and screenplays; worked as a fisherman, lives near St Combs.

Stan Gerry

Grew up in Portsoy, lives near Fraserburgh. Worked in the Canadian Arctic, writes poetry and stories.

George Gunn

Caithness poet and playwright, first writer in residence for Banff and Buchan.

Haworth Hodgkinson

Founder member of Peterhead Writers' Group, now in Dundee.

Anne McCabe

Lives in Strichen.

Mary MacCall

From Fraserburgh, her novel is set there.

Angus MacDonald

From Fife. Lives in Sandhaven.

Duncan MacLean

From Fraserburgh. Widely published novelist and short story writer.

Ian Morrison

From Laurencekirk, works in Banff, lives in Gamrie. Published poet and fiction writer.

Marjory Nicholson

From Turriff, lives in Macduff. Author of the collection Ah Wish ah Hid a Fiver.

Christine Ritchie

From the Black Isle, lives near Fraserburgh.   Has published poetry and stories and a collection, Moraine.

Michael Ross

From Aberdeen, lives in Peterhead.

Morag Skene

From Aberdeen, lives near Peterhead.

Bill Sluyter (pronounced 'Slooter')

Aberdonian of Dutch descent, lives in Macduff. Writes poetry and fiction. Legendary Aberdeen football supporter.

Alexander Smith

Lives in New Pitsligo.

Grainne Smith

From Keith, lives in Macduff, works in Fyvie. Writes poetry, fiction and drama.

Kathleen Smith

From Buchan, teaches in Gamrie, writes in Scots and English.

Robert Stephen

From Cairnbulg, former fisherman and teacher; paints local scenes, enthusiastic local historian.

Jean Tarras

Lives near Banff. Belongs to Turriff and Banff writers' groups.

Irene Tavendale

From Aberdeen, lives in Banff.

Sheena Young

Lives in Portsoy; playwright and drama worker.